W9-BCA-957

When a Loved One Leaves the Church

Lorene
Hanley
Duquin

Our Sunday Visitor Publishing Division
Our Sunday Visitor, Inc.
Huntington, Indiana 46750

Scripture verses cited in this work are taken from the *Revised Standard Version, Catholic Edition*, copyright © 1965 and 1966 by the Division of Christian Education of the National Council of the Churches of Christ in the U.S.A. and are used by permission of the copyright owner. Every reasonable effort has been made to determine copyright holders. If any copyrighted materials have been inadvertently used without proper credit being given in one manner or another, please notify Our Sunday Visitor in writing so that future editions may be corrected accordingly.

Copyright © 2001 by Lorene Hanley Duquin

All rights reserved. With the exception of short excerpts for critical review, no part of this book may be reproduced in any manner whatsoever without permission in writing from the publisher. Write:

Our Sunday Visitor Publishing Division
Our Sunday Visitor, Inc.
200 Noll Plaza
Huntington, IN 46750

ISBN: 0-87973-940-1
LCCCN: 00-140000

Cover design by Rebecca J. Heaston
Interior design by Sherri L. Hoffman

PRINTED IN THE UNITED STATES OF AMERICA

To Tom, who never left.
To Betsy, who left and came back.
And to Maggie, who is still undecided.

When a
Loved
One
Leaves
the
Church

Table of Contents

Preface

Lorie Duquin is in love. She is in love with her husband, with her children, with God, with the Church, and with God's people. To everyone who knows her, it's transparent. To everyone who reads this book, it's self-evident.

The book is a gift. Share it as a gift. People will love you for it. But read it first. You'll find between the covers a whole family of loving people who offer wise and practical insights on life, spirituality, and religion.

It is Lorie's book, however, and she has done her homework. Some might call it research, but that would ring of the impersonal, and this book is eminently personal. Reeling off one real-life situation after another, the messages are both down to earth and uplifting, describing life as it so often is but suggesting higher aspirations as to what it might be.

Informed and informing, Lorie Duquin portrays the adventure of life as stories of people and relationships, grounded in our fundamental relationship with God. She offers in these pages an extraordinary gift, held together with ribbons of effervescent hope.

– Most Rev. Henry J. Mansell
Bishop of Buffalo

Chapter 1

When a Loved One Leaves the Church

~~~~

"The one thing I know is that it is a painful journey both for those who left and for those who pray for their return." — D.C.H.

A Divided Family

Cecilia Stack has seven grown children who were all raised in the Catholic faith. Only one is a Catholic in good standing. One is divorced and remarried without an annulment, but is raising his children Catholic. Four are active members of Protestant churches. The youngest practices no religion at all. "It was more important to him to be married on the beach than by a priest," Mrs. Stack recalls. "He says he has nothing against the Catholic Church. It's just not important to him."

In the United States today, there are an estimated 16 million to 20 million fallen-away Catholics.

Mrs. Stack prays that her family will eventually be reunited in the practice of the Catholic faith, but deep down inside she knows that it may never happen.

"You know what it amounts to?" she says. "It's that you're not getting to live out your dreams. When you're first married and having babies, you never think it will turn out like this."

The Stack family is not unique. In the United States today, there are an estimated 16 million to 20 million fallen-away Catholics. For the families and friends of the people who no longer practice the Catholic faith, it is not easy. Most of these people carry their pain silently. Some are too ashamed to admit that a family member or a friend is away from the Church. Others have questions and concerns but don't have the courage to ask. Some ask the questions but don't ever feel as if they receive satisfactory answers.

What to Say? What to Do?

People want advice on how to deal with teens or young adults who struggle with doubts. They are concerned, and sometimes embarrassed, by a spouse who won't go to Mass. They want to know what to say when a friend or family member insists that Catholics aren't saved because they don't accept Jesus Christ as Lord and Savior. They don't know what to say or do when a friend or family member tries to convert them to another faith. They worry about adult children entering mixed marriages. They agonize over unbaptized grandchildren.

"What do I say to my daughter who tells me she gets more nurturing and a deeper sense of spirituality in a Protestant church?"

Some people feel a part of themselves die when a family member embraces another faith or rejects religion entirely. "What do I say to my daughter who tells me she gets more nurturing and a deeper sense of spirituality in a Protestant church?" asks a distraught mother.

Others are afraid to face God. "I'm going to die soon," admits an 80-year-old man, "and I don't know how I'm going to explain why my sons don't go to Mass."

Some people wrestle with guilt. "We put our son through Catholic schools. We went to church every Sunday. But we must have done something wrong. He is now a Pentecostal missionary in South America."

Others seek simple answers to complex questions. "Can you tell me what to say to my sister who claims to be spiritual but not religious?"

Some want specific advice. "My son is getting married by a justice of the peace. My wife refuses to go to the wedding. Is that the right thing to do?"

Many reach a point where a kind of hopelessness settles in. "Out of my three grown children, only one is a practicing Catholic. My two daughters will tell you they are Catholic, but they haven't gone to Mass in years and their children are unchurched."

These people wonder if there is something they can do. They would like to know how other people handle similar situations. They want some assurance, some guidance, some support.

You Are Not Alone

Unfortunately, there isn't much attention focused on this problem. Programs designed to invite lapsed Catholics to return to the Church have emerged, but no one gives much thought to the people whose family members are away from the faith. There are no studies on the faithful Catholics who sit in the pews praying for their loved ones. No surveys. No statistics.

If you're reading this book because someone you love is away from the practice of the Catholic faith, you may already recognize bits and pieces of your story on these pages. That is the purpose of this book. It will give you the

Saints Also Struggled

For centuries, the story of St. Monica's prayers for the conversion of her son, Augustine, has served as a classic example of a mother's faith-filled perseverance. Most people are surprised to learn that some of the other saints faced similar difficulties with family members and friends:

- *St. Catherine of Genoa* (1447-1510) suffered great anguish over the unfaithfulness and immoral behavior of her husband during the first 10 years of their marriage. Her own faithfulness eventually led to his conversion and his membership in the Third Order Franciscans.

- *St. Thomas More* (1478-1535) stood firm in opposition to King Henry VIII's challenge of papal authority, a stance that would eventually cost him his life. During this agonizing time, St. Thomas More never disowned his son-in-law who held, for a time, equally strong views in opposition of the Catholic Church. In spite of their opposing views, his son-in-law was always welcomed into the More home.

- *St. Louise de Marillac* (1591-1660) agonized over her only son, who fell away from the practice of the faith, lived with a string of different women, and fathered a child out of wedlock. In an encouraging letter, St. Vincent de Paul reminded her that "Our Lord, in his wondrous Providence, allows children to break the hearts of devout fathers and mothers. Abraham's was

> broken by Ishmael, Isaac's by Esau, Jacob's by most of his children, David's by Absalom, Solomon's by Roboam, and the Son of God by Judas."
>
> • *Blessed Frederic Ozanam* (1813-1853), founder of the St. Vincent de Paul Society, lived in a boarding house with people who ridiculed his religious beliefs and practices. "I am the only one who keeps the fasts," he complained, "which has made me the butt for many a gibe."

opportunity to explore in a safe and private way some of the issues, questions, and concerns faced by other people in similar circumstances.

About This Book

The book is divided into three sections. The first section deals with some of the questions faced by family members and friends. The second section takes a deeper look at 12 specific situations that people encounter when a loved one leaves the practice of the faith. The third section looks at the reality of some people returning to the Church and others staying away. It offers practical suggestions on what family members and friends can and cannot do when a loved one begins to show interest in coming back to the Church, or when a loved one shows no interest at all.

Throughout this book, there are stories of people who have returned to the practice of the faith. There are stories of people who are still away and may never return. There are stories of how friends and families dealt with different circumstances. All of these stories are true, although some of the details may have been changed to protect the privacy of those who requested anonymity. While each experience is unique, you may find yourself relating to the feelings expressed. You may receive answers to some of your questions. You may be surprised to discover that some of the things you thought were true were really myths and misconceptions. You may come to rely on a new source of spiritual strength and support in a God of infinite mercy and love.

No Easy Answers

This book offers no easy answers, no simple steps, no surefire strategies, no guarantees on how to bring a loved one back to the Church. No one could do that anyway. The decision to return to the practice of the faith is part of a conversion process that no one — not even God — can force someone to make.

It's not easy when a loved one leaves the Church. Accepting the fact that you are not alone is an important first step. It leads to the deeper understanding that this is really a bigger and more complex problem than most people ever imagined.

Chapter Notes

Sidebar: *"Our Lord, in his wondrous Providence . . ."*: Vincent J. O'Malley, C.M., *Ordinary Suffering of Extraordinary Saints* (Our Sunday Visitor Publishing Division, 2000).

Sidebar: *"I am the only one . . ."*: Ibid.

The Questions

"Be patient toward all that is unsolved within you and try to love the questions themselves. The point is to live everything. Do not seek the answers that cannot be lived, but love the questions, and perhaps without knowing it you will live your way into the answers."

Rainer Maria Rilke

While there are different circumstances surrounding each person's story, there are several common concerns that people express when a family member or a friend leaves the practice of the Catholic faith. In the next section, we'll take a closer look at five heart-wrenching questions that are most frequently asked when a loved one leaves the Church:

- ❖ Why Do They Leave?
- ❖ Whose Fault Is It?
- ❖ Why Am I So Upset?
- ❖ How Can I Keep the Lines of Communication Open?
- ❖ What If This Person Is Dying?

Chapter 2

Why Do They Leave?

"You want to know why. It is the big question, and sometimes it's so hard to find out the real reason." — C.S.

Why?

At an evening of prayer, information, and reflection for people in the Diocese of Buffalo who were struggling with a loved one that had left the Catholic Church, nearly 200 people from all age categories clustered into small groups. After the opening prayer, participants were asked to identify the reasons people leave the Church. The question "Why?" hung over the crowd like a thick mist. Some people stared at the floor. Some sighed. Others shook their heads. A few admitted that they didn't know why family members or friends strayed away from the Catholic Church. "It's not something that we can have a calm, cool conversation about," one woman confessed.

A Long List of Reasons

Gradually, however, people began to share painful stories of loved ones who no longer practiced the Catholic faith. Some told how family members or friends had joined other churches. Some spoke of family members who seemed to have embraced their own private spirituality. Others described loved ones who refused to practice any religion at all. Some expressed concern over children, a spouse, a sibling, a close friend, or other family members who seem to have lost all faith in God.

Before long, the groups compiled a long list of reasons why people leave the Catholic Church. It included everything from "bored" and "busy" to "marriage problems" and "painful memories."

Interfaith marriage emerged as a key component. One woman sobbed as her husband explained that their son-in-law had finally convinced their daughter to join a Protestant church.

Tension mounted when the word "divorce" was added to the list. Some people believed that Catholics are automatically excommunicated when a divorce decree becomes final. They were stunned to learn that this is NOT true.

"Are you telling me that my daughter, who is divorced, can still receive Holy Communion?" one man asked.

"Yes," a priest insisted, "as long as she has not remarried without an annulment."

Lifestyles Opposed to Church Law

Marriage outside the Church loomed as a major reason that people leave the Catholic faith. "My oldest brother married in the Church. But after his wife left him, he remarried a divorced woman and joined a non-denominational church that preaches against Catholics," one woman admitted. "My older sister was married in the Church, but she got divorced and remarried two more times. She is now single and happy, but has never gone back to the Catholic Church."

Several people mentioned Catholic teachings on sexuality and abortion as issues that keep people away from the Church. "My sister says the Catholic religion is a religion of DON'T," one person said. "It is negative. Don't do this or that."

A good number of people had family members whose lifestyles were not in line with Catholic teaching. Couples living together emerged as a major concern. One woman, who had just learned that her son is gay, was too upset to state the reason, so someone else listed gay and lesbian issues for her. As soon as that happened, someone else noted that many parents of gays and lesbians have also left the Catholic Church.

Feminist issues arose. "My daughter no longer practices Catholicism because of what she calls its 'male supremacist' ideology," one man pointed out.

Others noted that a departure from Catholicism is sometimes associated with a recent death or some other anxiety-producing event. "After their son was killed in an automobile accident, my neighbors stopped going to church," one woman admitted. Another man explained how his boss ended up joining a Protestant church after his wife died. "No one in the Catholic Church seemed to recognize what he was going through. He told me later how hard it was to sit alone at Mass. Someone at work invited him to a non-denominational church and the people in that church helped him through a very difficult time. It took away some of the loneliness."

Faith Found in Other Places

The strong emotional support offered in some Protestant churches was cited as a major factor in drawing people away from Catholicism: "My children left because they liked the sermons and the family-oriented sense of community in a non-denominational church."

A few people said their friends or family members changed religions for theological reasons. Several people described the gradual distancing of family members and friends after attending what was supposed to be an ecumenical Bible study:

- "My neighbor went to one of those groups," one woman explained. "Before long she started telling me that she never learned about the Bible in the Catholic Church. Within a year, she had not only joined this other church, but she was trying to get everyone else in the neighborhood to join."
- "My children left the Catholic Church for the same reason," another woman confessed. "They like the way the Fundamentalists tell them that they are now saved and will automatically go to heaven. They like the idea that all the answers are in the Bible."

Problems with the Church

Other reasons for leaving included difficulties during confession, negative reactions to changes in the Church since the Second Vatican Council (1962-1965), and bad experiences with a nun, a priest, or a Catholic lay person. "My sister says Catholics are hypocrites," one woman explained. "The last time she went to Mass, she accidentally bumped into some woman on her way back from Communion and the woman gave her the dirtiest look. That was the straw that broke the camel's back. She now goes to a Protestant church where she says people are friendly and really care about you."

The Drift-Aways

Some people said their family members or friends just seemed to drift away. "There was no dramatic break with the Church over issues, no arguments with priests, no criticisms, no complaints," one man said. "It was just a gradual distancing until my son said he just didn't feel Catholic anymore."

"Often we Christians constitute the worst obstacle for those who try to become closer to Christ; we often preach a Gospel we do not live."
— MOTHER TERESA OF CALCUTTA

Others said their family members didn't leave the Catholic Church; they just don't go to Mass. Several women said their husbands lost interest.

For others, going to Mass was simply not a priority. "Little League sports has taken the place of religion for my son and my grandchildren," one man noted.

The impersonal nature of large suburban parishes with fewer priests was mentioned as a factor: "No one cares if they are there or not! No one even notices."

A teenager complained that her mother stopped going to church after her parents were divorced. "It left me with no one to go to church with," she said, "so I hardly go anymore because I hate sitting there by myself."

A significant number of people expressed concern over teenagers and young adults who refuse to go to church. "My kids don't have any negative feelings about the Catholic Church," another man pointed out. "They just don't feel like going to Mass. They say it's boring, and I have to admit that sometimes it is boring."

Five Categories of Fallen-Away Catholics

The list of examples could go on and on. In fact, there are probably as many reasons for leaving the Catholic Church as there are people who left. Twenty years ago, sociologist Dean R. Hoge compiled the most common reasons into five broad categories of fallen-away Catholics. These five categories still apply today:

1. **Family Tension Dropouts:** These people grew up with tensions in their families, and as soon as they were old enough, they rebelled against both the family and the Catholic Church.

2. **Weary Dropouts:** These people felt bored by the Church and stopped going when pressure from parents or a spouse ended, or when their children grew up and there was no longer a need to be a role model for them.

3. **Lifestyle Dropouts:** These people's lives do not comply with Church laws. They include couples who are divorced and remarried, sexually active homosexuals, unmarried couples living together, etc.

4. **Spiritual Need Dropouts:** These people find that their spiritual needs are not met by the Catholic Church. They are attracted to other religions for worship, prayer, Bible study, and a sense of community.

5. **Anti-Change Dropouts:** These people objected to changes in the Church after Vatican II. At first, people left because they felt that there was too much

change. Today, some people leave because they feel there was not enough change.

You can probably think of family members or friends who could fall into any of these categories. You may be able to add new categories or specific examples of your own. But knowing why someone left the practice of the Catholic faith does not always provide the answers or the assurances that you seek. You may find that as you uncover new insights or explanations for what happened, you begin to face new and more painful questions. You may start to wonder:

- Is there something I could have done to prevent this?
- Am I somehow responsible?
- Whose fault is it?

Chapter Notes

Twenty years ago, sociologist . . .: Dean R. Hoge, *Converts, Dropouts, Returnees: A Study of Religious Change Among Catholics*, United States Catholic Conference (The Pilgrim Press, 1981).

Chapter 3

Whose Fault Is It?

"I think, as parents, we always seem to feel that we have failed in one way or another." — L.L.

Is It My Fault?

When Msgr. Vincent Becker gives talks to people whose family members or friends have left the Catholic Church, he usually opens with the statement: "I'll bet most of you sitting out there think you're responsible because someone you love doesn't go to Mass or may have joined some Protestant church or got turned off to God."

People squirm. Tension mounts.

"Well," he continues, "I would be willing to bet that maybe 1 percent of the responsibility might belong to you. But 99 percent is probably not your fault."

He pauses while the audience absorbs his words. Inevitably, someone will say: "If it's not our fault, then whose fault is it?"

If Only . . .

The answer to that question is not simple. When we face major disappointments and losses, we tend to look for someone or something to blame. We want to point our finger at something specific. We begin to speculate: "If this had happened. . . . If that hadn't happened. . . . If I had done this. . . .

If I had not done that. . . . If he or she had done or said this or that. . . ."

Keep in mind, however, that this kind of speculation is not usually based on solid evidence. It is very difficult to prove direct cause and effect when you are dealing with human beings. There are usually too many variables involved – none of which are true in all cases.

We begin to speculate: "If this had happened. . . . If that hadn't happened. . . . If I had done this. . . . If I had not done that. . . . If he or she had done or said this or that. . . ."

For example, experts agree that people in interfaith marriages are more likely to convert to another faith than people in same-faith marriages. While this is true, it is not true in all cases. Many Catholics who intermarry remain faithful Catholics. Why some do and others don't is not always clear-cut, and the tension of not being able to place the blame on something specific remains.

Who's to Blame?

One of the greatest temptations for many people, but especially for parents, is to blame themselves when a loved one leaves the Church. Father John Catoir, a syndicated columnist and former director of The Christophers, remembers the difficulty he encountered in trying to console a woman whose son had become a Lutheran.

"This woman was devastated," Father Catoir recalls. "She considered it a great failure on her part because her son had left the Catholic Church. She believed that it was her responsibility as a parent to pass on the Catholic faith to her children. She blamed herself."

"What did I do wrong?" she kept asking. "Is there something I should have done?"

"Sometimes," Father Catoir told her, "the best you can do is not enough. St. Monica was deeply disturbed about her son, Augustine, who was a scholar and teacher of a pagan philosophy. Was Monica at fault? No! His headstrong nature, his intellectual snobbery, and his pursuit of his own pleasure led him in a direction that he eventually repudiated as error. She was upset and concerned about it, but it was not her fault."

Take that one step further and look at the life of Jesus. Was it his fault that the rich, young man walked away (Mk 10:17-22)? Was it his fault that Peter denied him (Mk 14:66-72)? Was it his fault that Judas betrayed him (Mk 14: 43-45)? Was it His fault that Thomas doubted (Jn 20:24-29)?

"Jesus doesn't take the blame for the actions of other people," explains Father Gary Bagley, youth director for the Diocese of Buffalo. "He doesn't ask, 'Where did I go wrong?' He doesn't see himself as a failure. He is sad, but he always respects the other person's free will. One of the things we need to do if we are going to respect another person's free will is not to take someone else's obligation onto ourselves."

"Growth begins where blame ends."

— FATHER JOHN POWELL, S.J.

Adults Are Responsible for Their Actions

Moral theologian Msgr. Angelo Caligiuri agrees. "The bottom line is that adults are accountable for their own decisions. I meet many people who are really fine Catholics. They raised their kids in a Catholic home, and they practiced their religion. When those kids leave the Church, the parents feel the pain deeply. They say, 'What did I do wrong?'

I tell them that they didn't do anything wrong. They fulfilled their responsibility. The only question parents have to ask themselves is: 'Did we do everything we could to share our faith with our children?' If the answer is yes, you are not responsible."

But what if the answer is no?

What If It Is My Fault?

Let's say a couple in their early years were not churchgoers. The kids grow up without going to church and without a strong foundation in the Catholic faith. Or maybe one parent went to church and the other didn't. At some point, the parents decide to make religion a priority in their own lives, and they want their children to go to church too. It might work if the children are young. If the children are already teens or young adults, however, it might be too late.

"You can tell your teenagers and young adults that you're sorry and try to start over, but don't expect that they will respond automatically or that everything will be fixed magically," warns Father Bagley. "If you didn't take your kids to the dentist for 16 years, it doesn't mean you're going to be able to take them now and have their teeth fixed right away. It may take a while and some of the damage might not ever be completely repaired."

"The sad part of my story is my daughter and my grandchildren," one woman admits. "During the period of time that I was neglecting my spiritual life, my daughter was being deprived of that beautiful foundation I had enjoyed as a child. Although she was baptized and received Holy Communion, attended Mass, etc., she didn't get the living example of family. She grew up with the changes of Vatican II that occurred while I was 'out to lunch.' I sent her off to church with anyone who happened to be going, paying no attention to the need for parental guidance. Today she is married out of the Catholic Church, has two beautiful children who are baptized out of the faith. My cross today is in knowing that her alienation from the Church is all a result of my indifference."

Parents are responsible for helping to form the conscience of their children. They are responsible for presenting the truth, for making sure their children are instructed in the faith, for giving good example, and for praying that their children will make good choices.

"If you think you are at fault for your children not practicing their faith, it is certainly an area that is legitimately spoken about in confession," explains Msgr. Caligiuri. "Whether or not you are guilty is another thing."

Guilt

Guilt is anger and disappointment that we direct toward ourselves when we do something that we think is wrong. There are two kinds of guilt. Bad guilt is often a misguided feeling of responsibility for something that is not really your fault. You wallow in bad guilt and beat yourself up for it. Good guilt moves you to the point of determining what went wrong, how much of the responsibility falls on you, and what you can do at this point to make amends.

"Your level of accountability will depend upon whether you understood at the time that your actions were wrong and whether you acted freely with full knowledge and consent," Msgr. Caligiuri explains. "A priest can help you determine that."

"I think my mother feels guilty," admits a Catholic woman whose siblings are both away from the Church. "She told me recently that she wishes she could have put us through Catholic school but she didn't have the money."

While parents are a major influence in the faith development of a child's conscience, they are not the only influence.

There's a good chance that this woman is experiencing what Msgr. Caligiuri calls "bad" guilt. When she made decisions about her children's religious education, she based those decisions on her financial resources, the information available to her, and the situation her family faced. She had no knowledge of what the future would bring. She did the best she could at the time. She is only accountable for doing the best she could under the circumstances.

In assessing your accountability, it is important to remember that while parents are a major influence in the faith development of a child's conscience, they are not the only influence. Children also gather information and become influenced by other sources, including the Catholic Church, school, friends, the media, the entertainment industry, and society in general.

Good and Bad Influences

Sometimes, these influences draw people closer to Jesus Christ and the Catholic Church. For example, positive experiences in the parish community can strengthen people's relationships with Jesus, with the Church and with other people. The things young people learn in school can reinforce what they believe about God and all of creation. Friends can serve as positive influences that help to deepen a person's faith and commitment to serving others. The messages that come from the entertainment industry, the media, and society can challenge people to make a firmer commitment toward what they believe is true from a faith perspective.

Other times, however, these same influences can draw people away from the practice of the Catholic faith.

Problems with the Church

"I've often found that when people leave the Church it's usually not because of doctrine or specific issues," explains Father Joseph Burke, S.J., a psychology professor at Canisius College in Buffalo, N.Y. "They leave because somehow they haven't been able to connect. Maybe someone hurt them or something turned them off. It doesn't have to be a person in the Church. It could be someone or something that represents the Church. Maybe they feel that there is hypocrisy there. They react to what someone says or does. They begin to hurt, and they blame the Church because of something an individual does."

Mary Amlaw, a Catholic writer from Kennebunkport, Maine, agrees. "Much of what we fault the Church for is personal: a boring homily, music we find distasteful, annoyance with the congregation," she says. "Or we have a run-in with a priest or feel our efforts are unappreciated or the parish council doesn't support our pet projects. We translate human feelings of disappointment into spiritual causes and tell ourselves the Church is at fault."

Sometimes, it is a single event:

- "A priest refused to baptize my children because their father was Jewish," one woman says. "I was furious and stayed away from the Catholic Church for years. I never went to another church. I felt as if I were in the wilderness."

More often, it is a collection of negative experiences that build to the point where a person moves away from the Catholic Church:

- "Most of my bad experiences took place in the pre-Vatican II era," one man admits. "I have little more than bad memories, and it is a chapter of my life that I have put behind me. I know the Church has changed, and I know it is filled with many good people. I simply feel no need or desire to ever be part of the Catholic Church again."
- "I don't think the Catholic Church puts member participation high on its lists of important things," says a woman from New Jersey. "The pastor very often unilaterally determines what the parish will or will not do. As a result, many people with a lot of energy and enthusiasm have to go to Protestant churches where they can more effectively use their talents for God. The hierarchical structure stifles the action of the Holy Spirit in many communities. Ultimately, the doers move on, and you are left with a high percentage of people who want to be spoon-fed their faith and don't want to be challenged or even be particularly active."

Does the Church Care?

Some people question whether or not the Catholic Church really cares whether people come back. "I believe the role of the Church and the priest is to remove barriers for people to get to God, not to impose them," one woman explains. "In some cases, this is not being done. Some people have to jump though hoops. Others desperately want the sacraments but can't live up to the Church's expectations and leave in disgust. I always wonder if God will condemn those who have put up the barriers or those who flunked the Church's tests of worthiness."

> **"It would scarcely be necessary to expound doctrine if our lives were radiant enough. If we behaved like true Christians, there would be no pagans."**
>
> — BLESSED POPE JOHN XXIII

Questions have also arisen as to whether the Catholic Church has done a good enough job in instructing children in the faith.

"My pastor said that with Vatican II the teaching of our basic Catholic faith to children went out the window," says a man from Delaware. "Since these basics were missing, many people who were educated after 1965 seem to have lost their faith today."

Others disagree. "The Church may be responsible for teaching the Catholic faith, but I do not believe the Church is responsible for a person's faith or lack or faith," another man insists.

The Blurring of Religious Differences

Studies seem to indicate, however, that in recent years there has been a gradual blurring of lines among Christian denominations that can weaken a person's connection to a particular religion. In a 1999 poll of teens by researcher George Barna, more than half agreed with the statement "All religious faiths teach equally valid truths."

Jennie, a young adult in her mid-20s, says this is exactly what she was taught to believe. "We grew up in what I call 'mediocre Catholicism,' " she says. "In our parish, we would sing Peter, Paul and Mary songs at Mass. There was no crucifix over the altar, no statues in the Church. No one taught us what differentiated Catholicism from the Protestant churches. It was like they wanted to downplay the dif-

---

Are All Religions Equal?

A 36-page Vatican document issued by the Congregation for the Doctrine of the Faith during the summer of 2000 asserted the primacy of the Catholic Church over all other religions. The document, titled "*Dominus Iesus*: On the Unicity and Salvific Universality of Jesus Christ and the Church," emphasized that the Catholic Church is not merely "one way of salvation alongside those constituted by other religions." It reinforced traditional Church teaching that the Catholic Church was founded by Christ as "the instrument for the salvation of all humanity." While acknowledging "sincere respect" for other religions of the world and recognizing that non-Christians can be saved through a special grace that comes from Jesus Christ, the document emphatically ruled out "religious relativism which leads to the belief that 'one religion is as good as another.' "

---

ferences. I think many of us got the idea that Catholicism was interchangeable with any other religion. This made us very vulnerable whenever our religion was challenged by Protestant friends."

Peer Pressure

Some people say the influence of friends is a major factor in drawing people away from the Catholic faith:

- "I live in a part of the country where Catholics are a very small minority (about 5 percent of the population). I was constantly told by my Fundamentalist friends that Catholicism wasn't true to the Bible. No one ever told me different, so it was very easy to convince me."
- "I left the Catholic Church after a friend, who had been a devout Catholic, became a Jehovah's Witness. She witnessed to me and I loved everything that I read. I learned the hard way that the 'gospel' that they were preaching was not the Gospel of Jesus Christ."
- Patrick Levis, one of the stars in the action drama *So Weird*, which airs on the Disney Channel, admits that one of his friends tried to draw him into New Age. "He was telling me, 'This is something you could have more faith in. This is tangible.' "

Incidents like these raise the question as to whether Catholics are strong enough in their faith to resist attempts to draw them away. "Many times I wonder about that question and the different ramifications," admits Msgr. Vincent Becker. "In my parish, we have a Catholic school and a religious education program, but I ask myself many times, 'Have we really brought the children to a point of a real personal relationship with Jesus?' We talk about it enough that it would not be unheard of, but have we done it? I think we have to keep asking ourselves if we are challenging our people to make that personal commitment to the Lord."

The Impact of Secular Humanism

The rise of secular humanism in our society and in our schools is often mentioned as a factor in people falling away from the Church. It taught that you can still be a good human being, with sensitivity for the poor, without having anything to do with religion. You can be a compassionate humanist.

"I attribute a lot of the problem to a values-clarification course that was introduced in many public schools," says Father John Catoir. "It taught kids that they should make up their own minds about faith, ideals, values. The course was extensively trying to say that we are not going to influence what you decide. You are the one who must decide. Therefore, you have to examine carefully what your parents are teaching you and not take everything hook, line, and sinker. Young people got permission from their teachers to examine their parents, who are always suspect anyway because kids are in rebellion and they want to be on their own. They got fortified in a new way of thinking that was not present before the last century."

As respect for the authority of parents, clergy, and even teachers began to erode, moral relativism, self-indulgence, and subjectivity took root and became reinforced in popular self-help books. For example, in *Your Sacred Self*, author Wayne Dyer tells his readers, "You are sacred, and in order to know it you must transcend the old belief system you've adopted."

This focus on the "self" makes the individual the sole authority in all areas of life, with no respect for tradition, experience, restraint, or even truth. It is a key factor in what experts are calling "self-defined spirituality," as a replacement for "church-based" faith. Statistics from the National Opinion Research Center show that the number of people who claim no religious preference has climbed from 6 percent in 1972 to 14 percent in 1998. A recent poll by *USA Today* shows that 30 percent of Americans call themselves "spiritual but not religious."

"I can go on a 40-mile bike ride and get as much from it as I can from going to church," says Stephen Kelley of Brooksville, Fla., who grew up in the Catholic Church but rarely goes anymore. "Nature to me is what God is all about. It's a renewal."

Some say all these factors have contributed to a general moral decline in Western civilization. "Between the 1960s and the 1990s, disapproval of the state of America's morality has climbed 20 percentage points, and millions of adults in this country increasingly speak of a state of moral ennui that permeates many sectors of the general population," a recent Gallup Poll reports. The study shows that 62 percent believe moral values will be worse in 2025 than they are to-

"In the developed countries, there is a poverty of intimacy, a poverty of spirit, a loneliness, a lack of love. There is no greater sickness in the world today than that one."

— MOTHER TERESA OF CALCUTTA

day. They blame the media, the entertainment industry, and sensational scandals involving politicians, celebrities, and sports figures. Four in five adults expressed dissatisfaction over the general decline in honesty and ethical standards of behavior in the United States.

Culture Crisis

Education specialist Vincent Ryan Ruggiero insists that mass culture — fueled by media, advertising, and the entertainment industry — is a major factor in the erosion of moral standards and value systems that were respected by previous generations. He cites nine examples:

- In opposition to active living, mass culture promotes a spectator mentality and a desire to be entertained.
- In opposition to objective truth, mass culture extols subjective, design-it-yourself reality: "If I believe it, then it is true for me."
- In opposition to achievement through effort, mass culture promotes achievement through proclamation: "I am good, I am talented, I am wonderful."
- In opposition to informed opinion, mass culture suggests that all opinions are equally meritorious.
- In opposition to a demanding moral standard, mass culture extols doing whatever feels good.
- In opposition to intellectual activities, mass culture teaches that the only satisfying activities are those that dazzle the senses.
- In opposition to improvement through constructive change, mass culture promotes accepting and asserting one's self and inflicting self on others.

- In opposition to thinking, mass culture (particularly the advertising industry) plays on the public's needs and desires, and it prompts people to suspend critical judgment and accept biased testimony as fact.
- In opposition to self-discipline, mass culture lauds immoderation and lack of restraint.

Why Are Some Affected and Not Others?

These kinds of cultural influences don't affect all people in the same way. It's not uncommon to find siblings from the same family, with the same parents and the same religious upbringing, adopting completely different attitudes toward God and religion. "My sister was married in the Catholic Church," one woman explains. "Her husband went to Catholic school. Their kids were baptized, but they only attend church for special occasions like weddings. I talked to her once about going to Mass. She said she doesn't even think there is a God. She and her husband believe that religion is useless. She even told me that she didn't want me to raise their two daughters Catholic if something happened to them and we were to get the girls."

There's no good explanation why some people seem to have a naturally high degree of faith, while others are more skeptical or reject faith entirely. Maybe it is due to differences in personalities or temperaments. Maybe it is due to different attitudes toward life or life experiences. Sometimes, even the person who turns away from the Church can't identify a cause or find anyone to blame.

"I can't understand why it is so easy for my parents and my sisters to believe and it is so hard for me," one man confesses. "I'd like to believe, but I can't. I really struggle, while they just seem to accept everything without any questions or doubts."

So Who's to Blame?

Whose fault is it? Only God can look into people's hearts and answer that question. In most cases, a person's decision to stop practicing the Catholic faith can probably be attributed to a combination of influences.

"People who can believe should be a little more tolerant with those of their fellows who are only capable of thinking. Belief has already conquered the summit which thinking tries to win by toilsome climbing."

— C.G. JUNG

If someone you love is in that situation, don't take all the blame on yourself. It's probably not your fault.

"My parents were blaming themselves," one woman admits. "They thought it was something that they did to cause me to leave the Catholic Church. I would say over and over again, 'It's not anything you did. This is my choice. I am at peace in the Wesleyan Church. It is not what you did or didn't do. It had nothing to do with you. It wasn't bitterness or retaliation. It was simply going where I wanted to go."

In the final analysis, finding someone or something to blame doesn't really help. If fact, some people say it makes the situation even more difficult.

Chapter Notes

"The sad part of my story . . .": Christopher M. Bellitto, *Lost and Found Catholics* (St. Anthony Messenger Press, 1999).
"Much of what we fault the Church for is personal . . .": Mary Amlaw, "Why I Stay in the Catholic Church," *Liguorian* (August 1993).

"All religious faiths teach equally valid truths . . .": John Leland, "Searching for a Holy Spirit," *Newsweek* (May 8, 2000).

"He was telling me, 'This is something you could have more faith in . . .": Cynthia Hopkins, "What's Important to Patrick Levis," *Catholic Digest* (October 1999).

"You are sacred . . .": Wayne Dyer, *Your Sacred Self* (Harper, 1995).

"Statistics from the National Opinion Research Center . . .": Cathy Lynn Grossman, "In Search of Faith," *USA Today* (Dec. 26, 1999).

"A recent poll by USA Today shows that 30 percent of Americans . . .": Ibid.

"I can go on a 40-mile bike ride . . .": Ibid.

"Between the 1960s and the 1990s, disapproval of the state of America's morality . . .": George Gallup, Jr., and D. Michael Lindsay, *Surveying the Religious Landscape* (Morehouse Publishing, 1999).

"In opposition to active living . . .": Vincent Ryan Ruggiero, *Changing Attitudes* (Allyn and Bacon, 1998).

Quotation: *"People who can believe should be a little more tolerant . . ."*: C.G. Jung, *Psychological Reflections*, edited by Jolande Jacobi and R.F.C. Hull (Princeton University Press, 1970).

Chapter 4

Why Am I So Upset?

"If someone in the family does some other thing, like not following in the family business or breaking away from a family custom or tradition, it does not seem to have the same heinous quality as leaving the Catholic Church." — M.W.S.

Breaking With the Family

It's not uncommon to hear priests say, "One of the most heartbreaking experiences that I have with my parishioners is when they tell me that a family member or a friend no longer practices the Catholic faith."

Traditionally, religion has served as an integral part of the heritage, culture, and value system that families pass on from one generation to another. In fact, the word "religion" comes from the Latin root *ligare*, which means "to connect." If you are Irish, Polish, Italian, or Hispanic, it is generally assumed that you are Catholic. The identity of some families is so interwoven with Catholicism that a rejection of the Catholic faith is perceived as a rejection of the family itself. When this happens, the pain people feel is very real and almost always evokes a wide range of emotions. Sometimes, it's hard for people to identify exactly what emotions they feel.

"I am saddened by the fact that some of my family left the Church and joined the Unitarians," one person confessed. "I have read about the Unitarians and am so upset that they denounce the divinity of Christ that I am becoming too confused about it all."

Look at the range of feelings: Sad . . . Upset . . . Confused.

Emotional Reactions

Feelings are never static. In fact, it's not uncommon for one feeling to start an emotional chain reaction. Sadness and deep disappointment very often give rise to anxiety or feelings of frustration. Confusion enters the picture when someone's rejection of the family religion raises uncomfortable questions or doubts about what the Catholic faith really teaches and what the members of the family really believe.

"I am not made or unmade by the things which happen to me but by my reaction to them."

— St. John of the Cross

"I am concerned and maybe a little angry that my brother does not accept what our parents taught us," one woman admits. "I try to rationalize it by thinking that maybe he is not intelligent enough, but I still feel that it is an insult toward my parents."

Anger often triggers resentment, and tensions grow. It's not uncommon for people to begin to see a fallen-away family member as disloyal. They see this person as having broken the connection, and they feel as if this person has betrayed the entire family. "How could my son and his wife reject something that is so important to us?" one man asked.

Fear

As the emotional reactions continue, fear almost always enters the picture. In fact, dealing with a loved one who left the Church very often triggers the three greatest fears people face:

1. **Fear of abandonment:** Family members may begin to express concern about how this situation will impact family relationships:
   - Will it affect the way the family celebrates holidays and special occasions?
   - Will family members be able to relate to grandchildren, nieces, nephews, and cousins who are being raised in another faith?
   - Will it cause divisions in the family?
   - Will family members begin to distance themselves?

"My sister and her husband will not attend family First Communions or confirmations because they don't want their children exposed to Catholic rituals," one man explains. "It has driven a wedge through the core of our family."

2. **Fear of death:** Family members may begin to express concerns about what will happen to them or to their loved ones after they die:
   - How will God judge them?
   - How will God judge us?
   - Will we all be together for eternity?

The situation is compounded when family members or friends convert to churches that promote the idea that Catholics are not saved. "When my father was dying, my brother and sister were preaching to my father about how he wasn't going to heaven because he didn't accept Jesus Christ as his Lord and Savior," a young woman recalled. "My father was so hurt and upset. It was terrible. Religion has really become a source of conflict in our family."

3. **Fear of failure:** Family members may begin to see this situation as a failure on their own part or on the part of the person who left the Church:
   - How could he or she do this to us?
   - How could this happen?
   - What went wrong?
   - What did we do to deserve this?
   - What will people say?

Fear of failure is the least rational because it usually focuses on what other people will think or say. "All of this is so humiliating," one woman admitted. "We were always known as the perfect Catholic family. I can just hear people saying, 'Well, I guess they weren't as good as we thought they were.' " This fear of failure often fuels feelings of shame, which is one of the most insidious and debilitating emotions. People who are consumed by fear of failure may talk about feeling guilty, but what they are really feeling is shame.

Guilt and Shame

There is a big difference between guilt and shame. Guilt places blame on a person's action ("I did something bad!"). Shame puts the blame on the individual or the family ("I am bad!" "We are bad!"). The only way to deal with shame is to trace it back to its roots. Ask yourself: "Where is this negativity that I feel toward myself or my family coming from?"

Sadie Fletcher got caught up in feelings of shame when her teenage son refused to go to Mass with the rest of the family. "I came from strong Catholic Palestinian roots," she explains. "My ancestors were walking with the Lord in Palestine 2,000 years ago and being converted to Christianity. Our faith was so strong. My father came over here because Catholics were being persecuted in Lebanon. I kept thinking, 'How can my son not feel the same about going to Mass and receiving the Lord in the Eucharist as I did when I was his age?' I felt that there must be something wrong with me. I figured that I must not be a holy person if I could not convince my son to go to Mass — not just willingly, but wanting to go and desiring to go! It was all on my shoulders. What kind of a mother was I? I was not good enough!"

Anger and Control

Sadie tried to force her teenage son to go to Mass. He resisted by perfecting the art of stalling. "The family would be in the car waiting for him and I would get so angry," Sadie admits. "I would go back inside and I'd say, 'You're holding us up!' He would tell me to leave without him, but I was bound and determined that he would go. It was a struggle of the wills. One day I was so angry that I grabbed him by the legs and pulled him out of bed!"

The cycle stopped when a close family friend, Archbishop Joseph Raya, came to visit for the weekend. "Does this make sense?" Sadie asked him. "Is this what the Lord wants? I force John to go to Mass and then I don't pay any attention at Mass because I'm so angry. I am upset all day."

Gently, Archbishop Raya asked Sadie, "Don't you think God loves John just as much in bed as he does when he's at

Mass? Next Sunday, knock on his door and invite him to come. If he doesn't want to come, then just go to Mass and don't get angry."

Sadie says Archbishop Raya's advice defused the situation. "I got permission from the archbishop to invite John in the same way that God invites us. It took a big burden off my shoulders. It gave me a freedom that I can't describe. The burden was no longer on me. It was on the Lord. I started to pray, 'Okay, Lord, he's your problem. I've done everything that I could do.' "

> **"Have patience with all things, but first of all with yourself."**
>
> — St. Francis de Sales

Several years later, John Fletcher admitted that he was astounded when all of a sudden, his mother started knocking on his door and sweetly saying, "We're leaving for Mass in a half hour, John, if you want to come." The first Sunday, he stayed in bed, but the next Sunday he came. It was no longer a struggle. It was a choice. Today, he is studying for the priesthood.

God Never Forces

In the parable of the prodigal son (Lk 15:11-32), Jesus illustrates the unconditional love of God, but we tend to focus so much on the dramatic return of the prodigal son that we sometimes overlook the powerful example of how the father allowed his son to leave. The son's outrageous request for his inheritance and his plans to leave for a distant country were, in effect, saying that he wished his father were dead.

"The evangelist Luke tells it all so simply and so matter-of-factly that it is difficult to realize fully that what is happening here is an unheard-of event: hurtful, offensive, and in radical contradiction to the most venerated tradition of the time," explained the late author Father Henri J. M. Nouwen. "It is a heartless rejection of the home in which the son was born and nurtured and a break with the most precious tradition carefully upheld by the larger community of which he was a part."

The father could have refused. Instead, he gave the younger son his share of the estate and let him go. The father could not force his love on his son. He could not force his son to love him in return.

"He had to let him go in freedom, even though he knew the pain it would cause both his son and himself," Father Nouwen observed. "It was love itself that prevented him from keeping his son home at all cost. It was love itself that allowed him to let his son find his own life, even with the risk of losing it."

In Scripture, we see two other examples of Jesus letting people go.

> **St. Vincent de Paul offered the following advice to St. Louise de Marillac when she was agonizing over her son's lack of faith and immoral lifestyle: "Let him be guided by God; he is his Father more than you are his mother, and he loves him more than you do. Leave him settle it."**

When the rich young man walks away, Jesus lets him go (Lk 18:18-25). Jesus doesn't run after him saying, "Wait, maybe you don't have to give up everything. Maybe we could compromise." St. Luke tells us that Jesus was sad (Lk 18:24). St. Mark tells us that Jesus looked at the rich young man with love (Mk 10:21). But Jesus still allows him to walk away.

In the sixth chapter of St. John's Gospel, most of Jesus' followers walked away after he told them they must "eat the flesh of the Son of Man and drink his blood." Jesus did not run after them either. He turned to the Twelve Apostles and asked, "Will you also go away?" (Jn 6:22-71).

Letting Go

Letting go is one of the biggest struggles we face in every area of our lives. "I felt as if I were on an emotional roller coaster," one woman said. "I couldn't let it go. It kept eating away at me. I could not stop crying."

Crying is actually a good thing. Tears cleanse the body of toxins that are produced during times of stress and release a natural pain-relieving substance in the brain. Crying also discharges tension that builds up in your body. If you don't cry, that tension doesn't go away. So go ahead and cry, but remember that the point of all this crying is to let it go.

> "You need not cry very loud. God is nearer to us than we think."
> — **Brother Lawrence**

Whenever you let go of someone or something, you experience a loss. Your hopes, your dreams, your image of your family, and your plans for the future suddenly seem to crumble and die.

"The process of working through any kind of loss is essentially a grieving process," explains Sister Margaret Krantz, F.M.D.C., a certified bereavement counselor. "At first, you go through shock and denial. You refuse to accept that this happened. Then you may experience anger. You begin to ask: Why? What have I done to deserve this? Deep sadness — and sometimes depression — follows, until you finally come to acceptance, readjusting, recovery, and healing. You accept the fact that even if you don't like what's happening, you have no power to change the situation."

Sharing Feelings

It helps if you can find someone with whom you can share your feelings. This is not always as easy as it sounds. Part of the problem is that many people are afraid of their emotions and that they are afraid of sharing their feelings with others.

"Feelings aren't necessarily good or bad," explains moral theologian Msgr. Angelo Caligiuri. "Feelings are morally neutral. It all depends on what you do with your feelings. I might feel like punching someone in the nose, but if I don't act on it, and I integrate that feeling into myself, I become a more disciplined person."

"God commands you to pray, but forbids you to worry."

— St. John Vianney

Think of feelings as emotional energy. Talking about your feelings helps to dissipate the raw energy so that you can integrate the feeling. It is important to get those feelings out in the open. Repressed feelings don't go away. They stay beneath the surface and tend to erupt at the worst possible times.

Find someone who is a good listener. A friend, a relative, a priest, or someone else in your parish might be willing to help. You need someone to just let you talk without trying to solve the problem or offer advice. When you can freely talk about how you feel, there's less risk that you'll say or do something with friends or family members that you will later regret.

New Levels of Understanding

The more you talk, the more healing can take place. Try to move from what you are feeling to a deeper understanding of the thought patterns that are fueling those emotions. Subtle distortions in thinking can be difficult but not impossible to identify. Start by asking yourself, "Why am I feeling this way?"

The answer might be that someone you love has rejected God or the Catholic Church. But is it really your problem if someone else has rejected God or the Church? Isn't it God's problem?

So take it one step deeper. Are you feeling this way because you perceive that your family member or friend is rejecting you?

Think about that. Are they really rejecting you, or are they rejecting what you believe?

Now you have to face the question: "Are my beliefs strong enough to withstand someone else's doubts?"

This is not an easy process, but it can be worthwhile. "This is how change takes place," explains Jesuit psychologist Father Joseph Burke. "You move from the feelings to the thought process. What's the basis of the feeling? What's the thought process behind it? Is the thought process legitimate? What do you have to do to change those thought patterns? That's the challenge."

> **"To make good choices, I must develop a mature and prudent understanding of myself that will reveal to me my real motives and intentions."**
>
> **— THOMAS MERTON**

Father Burke believes that talking can also be used as a tool in breaking down some of the tensions that develop among family members. When you enter into a dialogue, you can begin to resolve some of the negative feelings and come to a deeper understanding of why the other person has chosen a particular course of action. The purpose of talking is to maintain the relationship even though there are differences of opinion. "It's very important to keep the lines of communication open," Father Burke says.

Chapter Notes

"The evangelist Luke tells it all so simply . . .": Henri J. M. Nouwen, *The Return of the Prodigal Son* (Doubleday, 1992).
"He had to let him go . . .": Ibid.

Quotation: *"Let him be guided by God . . .":* Vincent J. O'Malley, C.M., *Ordinary Suffering of Extraordinary Saints* (Our Sunday Visitor Publishing Division, 2000).

Chapter 5

How Can I Keep the Lines of Communication Open?

"At times I want to give up because it seems like nothing will happen, but something tells me to keep waiting, and eventually, my family will be reunited in one faith." — B.G.

God Is Love

Father Joseph Burke, S.J., remembers working with a Catholic family that was torn apart when one of the children decided to marry a Jew. The mother was on the verge of saying, "If you go through with this, you will no longer be a part of this family. You will not be welcome in this house anymore. You will be cut off." She insisted that she was taking this strong stand because she loved her child.

Father Burke asked her one simple question: "Do you think you love your child more than God loves your child?"

Because she was a faith-filled person, the mother answered, "No. God loves my child more."

Father Burke encouraged her to trust that if God loved her child as much as, if not more than, she did, then God would not leave this child alone. It helped the mother to see the situation from a different perspective. She withdrew her threat of disowning her child. She put the situation into God's hands.

"It's so unhealthy spiritually and psychologically to cut a relationship off," Father Burke warns. "That is negating the person. It's better if you can be open to dealing with the other side. When people care about each other, there has to be a certain tolerance of ambiguity. Even if you are right and the other person is wrong, it is important to keep the lines of communication open. You don't have to agree with what the person is doing. You can say that you don't approve. But don't sever the relationship."

"You cannot acquire the gift of peace if by your anger you destroy the peace of the Lord."

— St. Gregory the Great

Severing Relationships

There are actually two ways that people sever relationships. For some families, contact is cut off with a sharp and swift action that comes in a flash of anger. People say things without thinking. Communication comes to an abrupt and angry end when someone walks out. In other cases, the severing of a relationship takes place in four distinct stages:

1. **First, there is a gradual distancing.** "My mother cried and my father refused to talk to me because I had upset my mother," one young man explained. What appears on the surface to be a calm refusal to talk about the situation is really a passive form of withdrawal without any hope for resolution of the problem. Inwardly, people are churning with raw emotion.

2. **Both sides begin to talk about the problem with friends or family members almost as if they were staking out their ground and building a small**

army of support for their position. "My mother aligned all of my aunts against me," one woman says. "No one ever said a word, but I could feel their strong disapproval in their body language and in the tone of their voices."

3. **Negativity casts a dark shadow over everyone and everything.** People can no longer see anything positive about the person or the situation. People begin to think, "How could a son or daughter of mine do this to me? I can never trust this person again. I can never respect this person again. I cannot find anything about this person that I can love."

4. **Finally, one or both sides have built up enough psychological ammunition that they can justify cutting the other person off.**

Sometimes, people try nagging as an interim strategy. But that doesn't work either. Pressuring, berating, or telling a person what they are doing is wrong will only make things worse. "My mother tried that for a while," says Ann Sellers, who left the Church as a young adult. "It definitely doesn't work."

Another Alternative

Father Burke offers another alternative. It is called *detachment*. "Detachment is not cutting off the relationship," he says. "It is recognizing that you are not going to change this person. The process of detachment allows you to say, 'I don't know how this is going to be resolved, but I ultimately have faith that God will take care of it.'"

"I left the Catholic Church and attended the Assemblies of God and other Fundamentalist churches for 24 years," admits Mark Sturgis. "My mother, who is *very* Catholic, understood and supported my decision even though she didn't agree. She knew in her heart that Jesus would lead me back to the Catholic faith — and He did."

This is the essence of detachment. One way that you can reach the point of detachment is through dialogue.

A Chance to Talk

"Rather than have people throw barbs at one another, I ask them to talk about how they feel when the other person does this, or says this, or acts this way," Father Burke explains. "This allows people to focus on their own feelings. The dialogue is not intended to convince or to force someone to do something. The dialogue is to open up to a deeper understanding of what the other person feels."

It is never possible to force two people to reconcile. They must make that decision on their own. You can encourage. You can provide opportunities. But you cannot force. The only hope for some kind of resolution comes through dialogue. In using this technique, both sides have to be willing to listen. Keep in mind that the words that are being spoken are the smallest part of the communication. The tone of voice, body gesture, and attitude — all communicate more than the words.

You also have to be open to what the other person is saying. You have

> **"An interesting thing happens as we grow in intimacy and thus in transparency. We learn more about ourselves, as well as about the other. We become more fine-tuned and sensitive to our own inner states and thus have more to 'say' to the other."**
>
> **— FATHER WILLIAM A. BARRY, S.J.**

to recognize that some of the things that are said may be grounded in truth as one person experiences it. You may not understand that truth. You may not agree or be able to accept it. But you can accept that the other person sees this as being true for him or for her.

For example, a family member or friend might say, "I don't feel that in the Catholic Church I can spiritually connect to God or to Jesus in the way I can connect in a Protestant church." It might be hard to understand how someone might feel like that, especially if you have a deep belief and a strong devotion to the real presence of Our Lord in the Eucharist. But you still have to respect the fact that at this point in time, for reasons that you may never fully comprehend, the other person does not share your belief.

"We should, in my opinion, stop thinking of other Christian denominations as our arch foes and instead see them as less-perfected faith communities that are also on a journey," suggests one woman. "They do possess truths which we hold in common. We ought to share each instance where we come together so that the individual who has left the Church is not completely cut off from friends in the Catholic community. If we pray together that one day we will be one, then we have done all we can do. The rest is left to the Spirit of God."

Deeper Insights

Sometimes, in the dialogue, both sides discover that there is a deeper dimension to the situation that might not have been apparent at first. You may discover, for example, that religion has become the scapegoat for other problems in the family.

Father Burke remembers working with a family whose daughter was leaving the Catholic Church because she felt it oppressed women. It was complicated by the fact that her mother was somewhat oppressed by the father. When Father Burke asked the daughter if she could talk about her feelings with her parents, she looked at her father and said, "The Church for me is like experiencing what you do to Mom."

"It opened a can of worms, but a healthy can of worms," Father Burke recalls, "because, fortunately, the father did not jump all over her. They were able to talk about it, and it turned out to be a wonderful experience because the parents were able to hear what their daughter was saying."

You may not be able to enter into this kind of dialogue on your own. You may need a professional counselor or an objective third party to help keep the conversation focused. A third party can act as a referee by saying, "Let's not go there. Let's stay with this feeling. What did she just say? Can you understand what he is saying?"

It's important not to lose your temper or become defensive. "I have a brother who laughs openly about my faith," admits Sally Bishop of Montgomery, Ala. "About the only advice I can give is don't react to what they say or do. If they laugh, just smile and say it means a lot to you. Don't get mad. If they question you about why and what you believe, answer them fully and calmly."

Father Burke agrees. "What both sides have to strive for is empathy, which is really hearing what a person says

> **"Without mistakes, there is no forgiving. Without forgiving, there is no love."**
>
> **— MOTHER TERESA OF CALCUTTA**

and then giving back to the person the understanding of what they said," he explains. "It's more than just listening. People need to be heard. They don't necessarily need the other person to agree with them. You might reach a point where you agree to disagree. Agreeing to disagree is a legitimate step when people are trying to work things out. It leaves the question open. It sets up a boundary."

A middle-aged man from Houston, Texas, experienced this kind of boundary setting with his mother. He was away from the Church for 10 years. "At the time I left the Church, I was a non-committed person who had invested nothing," he admits. "When I was 18, my mother said, 'I took you to church for 18 years and I took you to catechism classes. Now you are responsible for your own faith.' She gave me ownership of my own faith. It was the best thing she could have done. Now I tell people, 'Never push.' Pushing a person will drive them into a hole. Putting the responsibility and ownership of the situation on a individual is respectful."

Leave the Door Open

Father Burke points out that this approach leaves the door open for people who are away from the Church to reconnect at some point in the future. "If you can say, 'I disagree with what you are doing, but I'm not cutting you off,' then you can continue to witness to what you believe with integrity," he explains. "You are not giving up. You are saying, 'We see things differently, but you are still my mother, my father, my spouse, my daughter, my son, my sister, my brother, my friend.' I think that's the healthy way to deal with this. It allows the people involved to have the sense that the relationship can continue. The breakdown of the relationship can lead to psychological and spiritual desolation, and that leads to hopelessness."

"None of my nieces and nephews has a strong faith in Jesus and our Catholic faith," says Arland "Buzz" Johnson of Delaware. "But I don't despair that so many have lost their way. I believe that our job is to love, to be good examples, and to pray. These are the things that will bring our children back."

Father Burke agrees: "Ultimately, people will say, 'I came back to the Church because my mother, my father, my relatives, my friends have so much faith. They accepted where I was at the time without ever stopping the witness of what they believe.' "

This approach worked in the life of Venerable Charles de Foucauld (1858-1916), who founded a religious community called the Little Brothers of Jesus. Charles was a profligate playboy. His cousin Marie de Bondy was a daily communicant with a special devotion to the Sacred Heart. Marie never shunned or reprimanded Charles. "She converted him without speaking a word," explains Father Vincent J. O'Malley, C.M. "It was her kindness and goodness that beckoned him."

Charles later acknowledged that Marie brought him back to Jesus. "I believed myself to have been damned," he told her, "when God enabled me to see in you God's goodness."

It's not easy to take this kind of approach, but it is the best way. The one question that remains in the minds of

> "At some ideas you stand perplexed, especially at the sight of human sin, uncertain whether to combat it by force or by humble love. Always decide, 'I will combat it by humble love.' If you make up your mind about that once and for all, you can conquer the whole world."
>
> — **FYODOR DOSTOYEVSKY**

many, however, is: What if my family member or friend is dying? At that point, isn't there something specific that I should say or do?

Chapter Notes

"She converted him without speaking a word . . .": Vincent J. O'Malley, C.M., *Saintly Companions* (Alba House, 1995).
"I believed myself to have been damned . . .": Ibid.

Chapter 6

What If This Person Is Dying?

"My father had a big fight with our pastor and stopped going to church a long time ago. When he was dying, he refused to let us call the pastor. He kept saying that the priest would never come. It was awful and we didn't know what to do." — C.M.

What Should You Do?

Deathbed decisions are difficult for every family, but it's even more difficult when someone you love has been away from the Church. It's not unusual for families to face last-minute questions that they may not know how to answer:

> "My life and death are not purely my own business. I live by and for others, and my death involves others."
>
> — THOMAS MERTON

- Do you ask a dying person if he or she wants to see a priest?
- If the person says yes, whom should you call? A hospital chaplain? A parish priest?
- What if the person is not registered in a parish? Would a priest come under those circumstances? What if a priest won't come?
- What if the person doesn't want to see a priest? Do you call a priest anyway? Would a priest come under those circumstances?

The Anointing of the Sick

From ancient times, the Catholic Church has maintained a tradition of anointing the seriously ill and dying with blessed oil. The early Christians were told, "Is any among you sick? Let him call for the elders of the church, and let them pray over him, anointing him with oil in the name of the Lord; and the prayer of faith will save the sick man, and the Lord will raise him up; and if he has committed sins, he will be forgiven" (Jas 5:14-15).

Throughout the ages, this special anointing became known as extreme unction or the "last rites" because it was often reserved for those who were at the point of death. This association of the sacrament with death resulted in many families feeling apprehensive about calling a priest for someone who was seriously ill because they didn't want to upset their loved one. Some people wanted to make sure the anointing would take place at the last possible moment before death as a kind of guarantee that the person would leave this world in a state of grace. It was not uncommon for people to wait until a loved one was unconscious or on the brink of death before calling a priest.

During the Second Vatican Council, the sacrament was revised, with emphasis on anointing people when they were seriously ill. The *Catechism of the Catholic Church* explains that "if a sick person who received this anointing recovers his health, he can in the case of another grave illness receive the sacrament again. If during the same illness the person's condition becomes more serious, the sacrament may be repeated. It is fitting to receive the Anointing of the Sick just prior to a serious operation. The same holds for the elderly whose frailty becomes more pronounced."

Today, the anointing of the sick is frequently offered on a regular basis in nursing homes, hospitals, and parishes, sometimes during a special Mass. It is also possible for a priest to administer the sacrament at the bedside of a person who is seriously ill.

"The Church has a history of charity toward the sick and the dying of which it can be unabashedly proud," insists author Mary Gordon. "The sacrament of Anointing touches that part of the broken body that doctors, social workers, and loving family and friends cannot approach: the part that, in order to be healed, must acknowledge its despair and travel from it to a place of hope. And this is what a sacrament must be: a vehicle for the journey between the seen and the unseen."

Recognizing the value of the sacrament is one thing. Talking about it with a seriously ill loved one, who has been away from the practice of the faith, is something else.

What Happens During the Sacrament of the Sick?

The sacrament of Anointing of the Sick is given to those who are seriously ill by anointing them on the forehead and hands with duly blessed oil — pressed from olives or from other plants — saying, only once: "Through this holy anointing may the Lord in his love and mercy help you with the grace of the Holy Spirit. May the Lord who frees you from sin save you and raise you up." — *Catechism of the Catholic Church* (no. 1513).

Offering the Opportunity

On the one hand, you may feel uncomfortable raising the subject because of a person's past hurts or problems with the Church. On the other hand, a person should always be offered the opportunity to reconcile with God. In fact, the *Catechism of the Catholic Church* insists that the family "should encourage the sick to call for a priest to receive this sacrament." If it's too difficult for you to raise the subject, ask a friend, a nurse, or another family member if they will pose the question.

Don't be discouraged if your family member or friend seems disoriented or makes strange requests. A person who is seriously ill or dying may not have the full use of his or her faculties. It's not unusual for people who are dying to make strange statements that seem out of character.

Msgr. David Gallivan remembers a very unnerving phone call when the father of a parishioner was dying. The family had asked the man if he wanted to talk to a priest. He replied, "Yes, but don't call that monsignor at Sts. Peter and Paul."

"They called me anyway," remembers Msgr. Gallivan, who spent the next hour searching – without success – for another priest who might have been able to come on short notice. When Msgr. Gallivan called the family back, they asked him to come because their father was in such a state that he would no longer recognize him.

"I anointed him," Msgr. Gallivan recalls, "and we had a moving prayer experience with the family around his bed. My offense never came up. If he recognized me, all was forgiven. To this day, I have no recollection of ever having met the man previously, let alone having offended him."

Finding a Priest

Start with your own pastor. Canon law says that one of the responsibilities of a pastor is to "come to know the faithful who have been entrusted to his care" and to "visit families, sharing the cares, worries, and especially the griefs of the faithful." He has a special obligation to "help the sick, particularly those close to death."

But keep in mind that pastors are often overloaded with responsibilities. If you can't get in touch with your pastor or one of the other priests in your parish, try a hospital chaplain, a Newman Center chaplain, or a religious-order priest stationed at a local school. You can also call your diocesan chancery for assistance in finding a priest.

If Your Loved One Says No

There is no clear-cut procedure to follow in cases where people say they don't want to see a priest. Technically, the sacraments cannot be administered against a person's will. But people who are dying may not have the full use of reason. They may be afraid that the priest will reject them. They may be afraid that God could never forgive them.

If you feel uncomfortable or unsure about the person's refusal, it's wise to contact a priest and discuss the situation. In the case of someone in a hospital or a nursing home, the chaplain can sometimes approach the person in a non-threatening way. If the person is at home, you may want to talk to your parish priest, who has probably had prior experience in dealing with these kinds of situations.

Father Tom Rowland remembers being called to the home of a man who was dying from cancer. "His marriage was not blessed by the Church, nor had he been to church in many, many years," Father Tom recalls. The man did admit to having been baptized a Catholic and to have practiced the faith as a child.

Father Tom was met at the door by a nurse who warned him that "this was one of the meanest, cussingest, most violent patients she had ever worked with." She doubted that Father Tom would even get past the door to his room.

She was right. When Father Tom entered, the man "yelled and screamed and told everybody to get out."

Father Tom refused to go. "After a while, he took a good look at me and he stopped yelling," Father Tom recalls. "He asked if anybody had turned me down yet."

Father Tom said no. The man replied that he would hate to be the first.

"He went to confession," Father Tom recalls. "I gave him the Sacrament of Anointing and went to the nearest

---

Prayers for the Dying

You don't need a priest to pray for someone who is dying. Whether you pray silently or together with other people, you can usually find comfort with the traditional Catholic prayers such as the Our Father, the Hail Mary, and the Rosary. Some people like to read passages from Scripture. You can also pray the Psalms. Here are a few suggestions:

- Psalm 23— The Good Shepherd
- Psalm 42 — Longing for God and Help in Distress
- Psalm 121 — Assurance of God's Protection

church to bring him Holy Communion. By the time I got back, everybody was flabbergasted. Having made his peace with God and with himself, he turned into the nicest person you could imagine. I brought him Holy Communion regularly for over six months before he died. His wife, won over by the effect the sacraments had on her husband, became a Catholic."

What If the Person Doesn't Reconcile?

You have no way of knowing whether or not a person has reconciled with God. You have no way of looking into a person's soul in the way that God does. You can't see all of the circumstances surrounding a person's actions or attitudes. You have no way of knowing what happens in the moments before, during, or after the soul leaves the body.

In the moments before Jesus died, the thief next to Jesus repented and Jesus promised the repentant thief that he would be with him that day in heaven (Lk 23:33-43).

Hospice workers say it is not uncommon for people in the last stages of life to have visions of Jesus, the saints, or loved ones that have died. There is always a chance that a person could reconcile with God in the final moments of life — even in the case of sudden death or suicide.

Pulitzer Prize-winning columnist Jimmy Breslin used to say that no matter how far from the Catholic Church

> **"If the greatest sinner on earth should repent at the moment of death, and draw his last breath in an act of love, neither the many graces he has abused nor the many sins he has committed would stand in his way. Our Lord would receive him into his mercy."**
>
> **— St. Thérèse of Lisieux**

people might stray, one chest pain and they go flying back to things they learned as children. "Nobody leaves the Catholic Church," he insisted.

Movie actor Jimmy Cagney left the Catholic Church after his father died in the Spanish Flu epidemic in 1918. Cagney got angry when the parish priest did not show up for the funeral, and Cagney stopped going to Mass.

During the later years of his life, Cagney's business manager, a lifelong Catholic, kept looking for ways to help him reconcile with the Catholic Church, with no apparent success. Before Cagney died in 1986, however, he told his business manager that he wanted a small Catholic funeral at St. Francis de Sales Church on East 96th Street where he had served as an altar boy many years before.

Did Cagney reconcile with God in those final moments? No one knows. The late Cardinal John J. O'Connor attended Cagney's funeral. At the end of the Mass, the cardinal apologized to Cagney's widow for the way in which her husband had been hurt by someone in the Church many years before.

Celebrity Funerals

Every time a Catholic celebrity who was not a practicing Catholic or held views contrary to Catholic teaching is buried with a Catholic funeral, questions arise as to who does and does not qualify for Catholic burial rites.

One woman was "very disturbed" over the attention given to international celebrity Giani Versace and Supreme Court Justice William J. Brennan during Catholic funerals. "To note, both had real problems with our Catholic faith," she wrote to the *Arlington* (Va.) *Catholic Herald*. "When I was growing up, I do not think these men would have been allowed to have been buried from the church. Is there any policy regarding this matter?"

Similar questions arose when former entertainer and U.S. congressman Sonny Bono, who had been divorced and remarried several times, was buried with a Catholic funeral.

The problem becomes compounded when a parish priest refuses Catholic funeral rites for ordinary people. This was particularly prevalent before Vatican II, but some families don't forget and pass detailed accounts of past hurts from generation to generation. Horror stories abound of priests refusing to bury ordinary people who were not registered in the parish, or did not attend Mass regularly, or did not keep up with their weekly envelopes. People who were divorced or married outside the Church were sometimes refused.

> **"You must see that no man should be judged by others here in this life, neither for the good nor the evil they do. Of course, it is lawful to judge whether the deeds are good or evil, but not the men."**
>
> **— *The Cloud of Unknowing***

"My grandmother's nephew was married twice and the priest would not bury him," recalls Msgr. William Stanton. "Suicides were never buried from the church. In some cases, they would have a service at the wake. People who were cremated were also not allowed to have any kind of funeral Mass."

Even though these restrictions have been lifted, it's not uncommon for people to agonize over loved ones who die while they are away from the practice of the Catholic faith.

They want to know who may and may not be buried from a Catholic church. They want to know what rights — if any — the family has in these difficult situations.

Before these questions can be answered, however, it is important to understand the meaning behind a Catholic funeral.

A Mass for the Dead? Or for the Living?

Before Vatican II, funerals were called the Mass of the Dead. Today, the emphasis has shifted to emphasize both the living and the dead. "Vestments have gone from black to white," explains Father William J. Bausch. "The phrase 'Christian burial' sounds a note of hope, and the white vestments hearken to the reality of the resurrection."

In fact, during a Catholic funeral, the Church asks "spiritual assistance for the departed, honors their bodies, and at the same time brings the solace of hope to the living." This threefold purpose is important. It means the funeral liturgy not only involves praying for the person who died and reinforcing the Catholic belief in the resurrection of the body but also serves as an opportunity to comfort the family members and friends who are grieving the loss of their loved one.

The instructions in the Order of Christian Funerals make it clear that "the celebration of the Christian funeral brings hope and consolation to the living. While proclaiming the Gospel of Jesus Christ and witnessing to Christian hope in the resurrection, the funeral rites also recall to all who take part in them God's mercy and judgment and meet the human need to turn always to God in times of crisis."

Father Francis X. Gaeta, pastor of St. Brigid's Parish in Westbury, N.Y., says the parish can make a tremendous impact on a family at the time of death. "It is a special time in which people are looking for a gentle and loving welcome home," he notes. "It is a time to heal past hurts and wounds. It is a time for the clergy and staff to become acquainted with families who have fallen through the cracks over the years."

Who Can Be Buried From the Church?

According to canon law, baptized Catholics are entitled to Christian burial. Canon law also notes that Catholic funeral rites can be granted to catechumens who are in the process of becoming Catholic, babies whose parents intended to baptize them, and baptized members of non-Catholic churches who desire Christian burial but whose own minister is not available. That means there are situations in which a non-Catholic spouse in a mixed marriage could be buried from a Catholic church. "I had a funeral one time for a man who was not Catholic," recalls Msgr. Stanton. "His wife told me that when he found out that we could do that, all the hurt from the past was taken away from him."

"Christ bids us to put love where we do not find it, and thus will we find everyone lovable."

— **Bishop Fulton J. Sheen**

In addition, people who commit suicide and people who choose to be cremated are no longer excluded from Christian burial.

Who Can Be Denied a Catholic Funeral?

Ecclesiastical funeral rites can be denied, but canon law is very specific as to the circumstances. "Unless they have given some sign of repentance before their death, the following are to be deprived of ecclesiastical funeral rites: notorious apostates, heretics, and schismatics; persons who had chosen the cremation of their own bodies for reasons opposed to the Christian faith; other manifest sinners for whom ecclesiastical funeral rites cannot be granted without public scandal to the faithful."

Who Decides?

Most lapsed or fallen-away Catholics would not meet these strict criteria as heretics and notorious sinners. The designation is usually reserved for people who have formally renounced the Catholic faith or were formally excommunicated. This happens very rarely. In most cases, it's not unusual for people to express some sign of sorrow or repentance before they die.

"I remember one young man with AIDS, who died in my arms," recalls Msgr. Stanton. "I remember going to the hospital thinking, 'This is tough. Will he receive me?' I remember praying hard that this boy would listen to me and we would be able to talk."

When Msgr. Stanton arrived, the young man was alone. "He began to tell me his whole story. At the end, I asked him if he would like absolution. He said, 'I'd like that.' "

A few days later, the young man took a turn for the worse. Msgr. Stanton went to see him. "The whole family was there," he recalls. "He

> **"No mother could be quicker to snatch her child from a burning building than God is compelled to bring help to a penitent soul, even if the person has committed every imaginable sin a thousand times over."**
>
> **— BLESSED HENRY SUSO**

was gasping for breath. He was hardly conscious. I said, 'John, let go. Jesus is waiting. It's going to be a wonderful experience. There's no more hassle. Jesus loves you. Let go.' "

Msgr. Stanton suggested that the family pray together. "We said the Lord's Prayer," he recalls. "I held his head in the crook of my arm. He died just like that. At the funeral, I told the story and there wasn't a dry eye in the crowd. It's a beautiful story. That's what priests do. We try to reach people and show them God's love."

When Questions Arise

When someone dies without some outward sign of repentance, the Church usually gives the person the benefit of the doubt. "When my brother-in-law died from a heart attack, our pastor refused to bury him because he was remarried to my sister without an annulment," one woman explains. "The pastor said it would cause scandal in the parish. My brother-in-law was a very good person, and they were in the process of applying for an annulment. My father called the bishop's office and arrangements were made to have the funeral in another parish."

When there is a question, canon law stipulates that the local bishop should be consulted and that his judgment in the matter should be followed. That means families who are refused the Christian burial of a loved one can appeal to the local bishop.

It's also wise to let another priest or the bishop know if you experience something that does not seem right to you. Father Flavian Walsh, O.F.M., recalls meeting a woman who stayed away from the Church for 15 years after the funeral of her brother. He returned from Vietnam and even-

"One of the keys to real religious experience is the shattering realization that no matter how hateful we are to ourselves, we are not hateful to God. This realization helps us to understand the difference between our love and God's."

— THOMAS MERTON

tually killed himself after a heartbreaking struggle with mental and emotional problems. After the funeral, the priest turned to the woman and said, "I don't know why we went through this charade of having a Mass. Your brother is in hell."

"This priest was wrong," Father Flavian insists. "He had no right to make that kind of judgment. No one can judge the state of another person's soul."

When Someone Doesn't Want a Catholic Funeral

"I had a friend who insisted up to the moment she died that she did not want a priest or a Catholic funeral," one woman recalls. "The family respected her wishes, but their parish priest suggested that the family have a private healing Mass a few weeks later for close family members and friends."

The greatest fears that people face when a loved one dies are these: Where did that person's soul end up? Are they suffering? Are they saved?

One of the most misunderstood doctrines of the Catholic faith is purgatory. It is sometimes helpful to look at purgatory not as a place of suffering and torment but as another stage on our pilgrimage to God where we resolve some of the things that were left unresolved at the time of our death. The concept of purgatory reveals the mercy of God, who gives us another chance to forgive, to repent more fully, to let go of old attachments, to turn completely to him in love and surrender. "Before we enter into God's kingdom, every trace of sin within us must be eliminated, every imperfection in our soul must be corrected," explains Pope John Paul II. "This is exactly what takes place in purgatory."

"I remember someone telling me that entering purgatory is similar to what would happen if you were invited to a dinner party and you showed up in casual clothes," one woman recalls. "But the other guests were wearing formal attire, so you get rid of your old clothes and change into new clothes before you enter the banquet."

Father John Mergenhagen, a lecturer and retreat master, tells grieving people that their family members and friends are probably happier in purgatory than they ever were here on earth because they have caught a glimpse of eternal life with God and they are preparing for union with God.

> **"The Lord is very loving toward human beings. He is quick to pardon, but slow to punish. Therefore, no one should ever despair of salvation."**
>
> **— ST. CYRIL OF JERUSALEM**

Praying for our deceased family members provides a spiritual link to them and keeps alive our love for them. It is a true test of our faith to put the lives of our loved ones – both living and dead – into the hands of God who is perfect love and infinite mercy. This kind of surrender is especially hard when we don't understand some of the dynamics surrounding a person's decision to leave the Church. In the next section of this book, we'll examine 12 tough situations that many people face and how they learned to live with them.

A Novena for the Dead

During his lifetime, St. Odilo (962-1049) served as abbot of the Benedictine monastery at Cluny, where he instituted the practice of providing "sanctuary" for people fleeing aggressors. His greatest legacy, however, was the institution of the feast of All Souls on Nov. 2, which he incorporated into his reforms of the monastery. The feast of All Souls remains an excellent time to remember deceased family members and friends by attending Mass and praying special prayers like the Rosary and novenas.

In his collection of novenas, Michael Dubruiel presents a novena for the souls in purgatory. The Novena for the Holy Souls includes the following prayers said once daily for nine consecutive days:

Let us Pray:

God, the Creator and Redeemer of all the faithful, grant to the souls of your servants and handmaids the remission of all their sins, that through our sincere prayers they may obtain the pardon they have always desired. Through Christ our Lord. Amen.

Lord God, by the Precious Blood which Your divine Son, Jesus, shed in the garden, deliver the souls in purgatory, especially those who are the most forsaken of all. Bring them into Your glory, where they may praise and bless You forever. Amen.

Our Father; Hail Mary

Eternal rest grant unto them, O Lord, and let perpetual light shine upon them.

May they rest in peace. Amen.

May their souls and the souls of all the faithful departed, through the mercy of God, rest in peace. Amen.

Chapter Notes

"It is fitting to receive the Anointing of the Sick . . .": Catechism of the Catholic Church, no. 1515.

"The Church has a history of charity toward the sick . . .": Mary Gordon, "Healing Holy Oil," in *Signatures of Grace: Catholic Writers on the Sacraments*, edited by Thomas Grady and Paula Huston (Dutton, 2000).

". . . should encourage the sick to call for a priest to receive this sacrament": Catechism of the Catholic Church, no. 1516.

". . . visit families, sharing the cares, worries, and especially the griefs of the faithful": Code of Canon Law, Canon 529.

". . . help the sick, particularly those close to death": Ibid.

The sacraments cannot be administered against a person's will: Code of Canon Law, Canon 1007.

"His marriage was not blessed by the Church . . .": Thomas Rowland, *God Acts . . . We React* (Madonna House, 1996).

"Nobody leaves the Catholic Church . . .": Peter Occhiogrosso, *Once a Catholic* (Ballentine Books, 1987).

Movie Actor Jimmy Cagney . . .: Michael Daly, "Gently Putting Right the Wrongs of Others," *New York Daily News* (May 9, 2000).

One woman was "very disturbed" over . . .: "Prudence Is Key in Judging the Dead," Straight Answers by Father William Saunders, *Catholic Herald*, Arlington, Va. (Aug. 21, 1997).

"Vestments have gone from black to white . . .": William J. Bausch, *While You Were Gone: A Handbook for Returning Catholics and Those Thinking About It* (Twenty-Third Publications, 1994).

". . . spiritual assistance for the departed, honors their bodies, and at the same time brings the solace of hope to the living": Code of Canon Law, Canon 1176.

"It is a special time in which people are looking . . .": Francis X. Gaeta, *From Holy Hour to Happy Hour: How to Build Christian Community* (Resurrection Press, 1996).

Baptized Catholics are entitled to Christian burial: Code of Canon Law, Canon 1176.

Catholic funeral rites can be granted to . . .: Code of Canon Law, Canon 1183.

"Unless they have given some sign of repentance . . .: Code of Canon law, Canon 1184.

"When there is a question . . .": Code of Canon Law, Canon 1184.
"Before we enter into God's kingdom . . .": Pope John Paul II, General
  Audience (Aug. 4, 1999).

Sidebar: *Novena for the Holy Souls*: Michael Dubruiel, *Mention Your
  Request Here: The Church's Most Powerful Novenas* (Our Sunday
  Visitor, 2000).

THE SITUATIONS

"Our life is full of brokenness — broken relationships, broken promises, broken expectations. How can we live that brokenness without becoming bitter and resentful except by returning again and again to God's faithful presence in our lives?"

Father Henri J. M. Nouwen

The reasons people leave the practice of the Catholic faith are as unique as the individuals involved. There are, however, several common situations that many families and friends face when a loved one leaves the Church. In this section, we'll take a closer look at 12 of the most difficult situations and some of the issues that surround them:

- ❖ Loss of Faith
- ❖ Spiritual But Not Religious
- ❖ Dabbling in Other Faiths
- ❖ Leaving the Catholic Church
- ❖ Interfaith Marriage
- ❖ Encountering Fundamentalists
- ❖ Cults
- ❖ Addictions
- ❖ Moral Dilemmas
- ❖ The Annulment Process
- ❖ Angry at the Church
- ❖ Angry at God

Chapter 7

Loss of Faith

"I am one of five children in my family. My parents were both devout Catholics and set a perfect example, but my two younger brothers never grasped the faith." — T.F.

A Joke That Isn't Funny

There's an old joke about three pastors who had pigeons in their bell towers. The first pastor tried to shoot them, but the pigeons came back. The second pastor tried to poison them, but the pigeons came back. The third pastor found a solution. "I asked the bishop to come over and confirm them," he explained. "The pigeons left and never came back."

Mike Murphy can relate to that story. He grew up in an Irish Catholic family. He went to Mass every Sunday until he was 14, but he didn't pay much attention to what was happening. "I really wasn't interested in the boring ramblings of a man I never met," he says. "I did what I was told. That's all. This explains my Communion and confirmation. I had no part in it – not consciously anyway."

After he was confirmed, Mike simply stopped going to Mass. It wasn't until he was in his 20s that he felt as if he wanted to "relearn what the Catholic Church and Jesus Christ are teaching."

"I have been talking with my family about our experiences," he says. "It appears that all my siblings (count eight) have experienced the same things that I have. The majority have returned or are returning to the Church. I am soon to follow, but have to meet with our local priest and be prepared for some major Hail Marys."

Mike believes that natural curiosity about the purpose of life and the desire to discover the reason we were placed on earth is what draws young people back. "I do believe there is a higher power at work, and I do believe that Jesus is the Son of God and that he died for our sins," Mike explains. "With that belief, I want to learn more. It has taken some time, but I had to create my own identity first. I appreciate my family's lack of pressure and non-interference. It helped me create my identity and start to really establish my values. Hard-core pressure would have surely driven me further away."

Losing Faith

Studies show that Mike's experience is typical. A recent survey confirmed that as many as 60 percent of young Catholics fall away from the Church during late adolescence and early adulthood. Some leave because of indifference. Others are too busy, or just plain lazy. Some disagree with Church teachings. Others adopt a lifestyle that is in conflict with Church rules. A significant number say they dislike their parish, the liturgies, the homilies, or a particular priest. Studies also show that most teenagers and young adults eventually turn back to religion.

While the experience of teens and young adults falling away from the Church may be fairly common, it's not much consolation to concerned parents:

- "My teenage daughter told me that she does not believe in the Catholic faith," one woman confessed. "She says she had never had a prayer answered."
- "I am the father of two great kids who graduated from Catholic high schools but seem to have lost their faith. I am concerned for their spirituality. I hope that God will eventually call them back, and I pray every day that we can share our faith together."
- "This past week my 28-year-old son told me he no longer believes in the Catholic Church," another mother admitted. "It was like a knife going into my heart, hearing his words. I think he falls into the 'I've been away for so long, I'm embarrassed to go back' category, so he rationalizes that it isn't relevant and that he doesn't believe it anyway. The bottom line is that he is too proud to return."

The Faith Journey

According to author and educator Father Mark Link, S.J., the process of turning away from religion plays an important role in a person's faith journey. The journey begins in childhood when a youngster accepts unconditionally the beliefs that parents and teachers have passed on. This is a very important stage because it gives children a history, an identity, a set of values, and a sense of belonging.

Childhood faith is very simplistic. It tends to be black-and-white without any room for doubt. Kids see themselves as being Catholic in the same way that they are Italian or Irish or Polish or Mexican. It is part of their family, their heritage, and their culture. There is no real ownership of childhood faith. Children follow along because it is part of family life.

During adolescence, a natural tradition begins that takes a young person from childhood faith to adult faith. It is a painful process when teenagers begin to question and doubt. Eventually, they reach the point where they're not sure what they believe. They feel alone and disoriented, as if a part of them is dying.

> **"Let me tell you this: Faith comes and goes. But if it is presumptuous to think that faith will stay with you forever, it is just as presumptuous to think that unbelief will."**
>
> **— FLANNERY O'CONNOR**

"I am utterly confused about my spirituality," admits 14-year-old Nicole. "I don't know why but recently I have doubted that God exists. I attend church and try to believe what is said, but I find it so hard. When I think about death, I get unbelievably terrified, thinking that if there is no heaven, where will I go? I picture it as just emptiness."

It's not uncommon for this adolescent transition period to stretch into the young adult years. "I am 28 years old," a young man says. "I was raised Catholic all my life, but left the Church because I don't know what I believe anymore. I felt like I had been following blindly for my whole life. There are so many things about Catholicism that I don't agree with or don't believe. I feel so lost. The Church once gave me direction, but I don't get that anymore."

Becoming a Committed Catholic

"The death of our childhood faith makes us feel sick of heart — even guilty," Father Link says. "This is unfortunate, for our faith is simply going through an important growth stage. It is changing from being a cultural faith to being a convictional faith."

In the process of moving from being a "cultural" Catholic to being a "committed" Catholic, young people take ownership of their spiritual lives:

- "Questioning what your parents have taught you is a natural part of growing up," explains a young woman in her 20s who went through the process. "We begin to ask ourselves if we are Catholics because our parents are Catholic or because that's what we really believe."
- "I had a similar faith crisis as a teen," another woman admits. "A priest suggested that I put everything on a mental back-burner and pray for belief. I had to work through what I really believe, a belief that was my own and not my parents'. This really is part of coming of age."

Three Levels of Faith Transition

According to Father Link, this adolescent transition takes place on three levels:

1. In the mind, where we begin our search for truth amid questions and doubts as to the nature of God and the various tenets of the Catholic faith.
2. In the heart, where we search for the real meaning of love in our feeble attempt to discover the truth that God is love.
3. In the soul, where we open ourselves to experiences of God that renew our faith and instill in us a willingness to make a personal commitment to a new way of life.

If the process is unsettling for teenagers and young adults, it can be even more disturbing to parents. "I remem-

> **"When a savage ceases to believe in his wooden God, this does not mean that there is no God, but only that the true God is not made of wood."**
>
> **— Leo Tolstoy**

ber one time a very upset woman came into the sacristy and told me her son had become an atheist," recalls Msgr. William Stanton. "He turned out to be a 13-year-old atheist, who was just questioning some of the things he had learned as a child. He threw the baby out with the bathwater, but it wasn't that hard to get the baby back."

Helping Young People Make the Transition

Family members and friends can actually help a teenager or young adult through this difficult stage, but they have to realize that there's a good chance they will become the scapegoat in the process. "A kid's frustration with religion will probably sound a lot like a kid's frustration with parents, relatives, or friends who are religious," explains Father Gary Bagley, youth director for the Diocese of Buffalo. "If you fall for that, you're done. You have to understand that the kid is working through some very valid and important religious questions. When teenagers or young adults express those questions, they may sound like they are attacking God or the Church or the family. You have to be big enough to know that it is not really a personal attack. You don't have to be defensive. You don't have to protect or insulate yourself. You don't have to have all the answers. You just have to listen."

Young people really do have a deep respect for their parents — even if it doesn't show sometimes. A recent study by the Barna Research Group found that 47 percent of teens say their parents have the greatest influence on their spiritual development.

"My parents never pressured me about the Church," says John Knutsen, who stopped going to church when he was 13 years old and spent the next 15 years in a state of rebellion and agnosticism. "I argued against religion whenever the subject came up and found truth in the writings of existentialist philosophers. I didn't know what I was talking about. My impressions of the Church were all based on media half-truths and the prejudices of friends who also knew nothing about it. My parents let me explore things on my own and that helped. I never would have responded to pressure or force. A young person is not likely to have a positive reaction if his or her family constantly brings it up and takes a disapproving line. My advice to parents and friends would be to back off, be available and supportive, and most of all, lead by example. Show the person through your own daily activities that there is much to be gained by staying in the Church."

Father Joseph Burke, S.J., agrees. "You can help them by the witness of your own life," he says. "They will see the meaning in your life, and they will want to reconnect because they want meaning in their own lives."

"I left the Catholic Church at the age of 19, not to join another church but because I ceased to believe," a young man confessed. "I returned to the Church 10 years later because I saw the way faith helped my family and friends through some very tough times. My own life seemed empty. I wanted the peace that seemed to come from their faith in God."

What Is Faith?

In a series of essays about the fundamental questions of life, author, theologian, and social commentator Michael Novak told his 24-year-old daughter that faith is not so much a "list of beliefs" as it is a new way of seeing the world.

"In faith, one does not see a different world," he explains. "It is the same world as before. But now one sees it in aspects that one had previously missed. One observes relations within it differently and — so it immediately seems — in their true light. The new light is more penetrating than any light you have experienced before. Suddenly you see the why of things, in a hidden code that now seems so obvious, and yet before was so unaccountably beyond grasp. Everything seems related. Many arrows, shot from many angles, converge: The Creator had a purpose. Everything speaks of God. The world is as it was. Yet it is no longer mute."

> **"Sometimes one who wishes to believe has more merit than one who does believe."**
>
> — St. Alphonsus Liguori

What Michael Novak is describing is a conversion process. Father Henri J. M. Nouwen described conversion as an inner event that cannot be manipulated but instead must develop from within a person. "Just as we cannot force a plant to grow but can take away the weeds and stones that prevent its development, so we cannot force anyone to such a personal and intimate change of heart," the late Father Nouwen noted, "but we can offer the space where such a change can take place."

The Process of Conversion

Father Joseph Gatto, an author and a theologian who works with young people who are discerning what God wants them to do with their lives, says a conversion involves a total redirecting of one's life. "It is a complete change of heart," he explains, "a complete reversal, a complete change of worldview and self view. It is part of the process of becoming spiritually mature. But it is not as simple as it may sound. I always tell people to look at conversion as a circle that is divided into four quarters. There is personal conversion, religious conversion, intellectual conversion, and moral conversion":

1. At the first level of conversion, a person asks the question: Who am I? "You begin to understand yourself in relation to the world, your family, your friends," Father Gatto explains.

   During a personal conversion, you start to see yourself as part of a broader mystery. You question your existence. You interact with the mystery of who you are and why you are here until you reach the point where you can say, "This is who I am in the midst of the world." There is no statement of God at this point, but a personal conversion leads you to begin asking questions about the ultimate meaning of life.

2. Religious conversion follows when you realize that you are not in control. All of a sudden, you see yourself as a creature, and you recognize that there must be a creator because you are fragmented. You don't have complete answers. You are finite. You will not live forever.

   "This is the beginning of a religious conversion," Father Gatto explains. "You admit that you are a dependent being in relationship to a larger mystery. The first thing it does is explode your image of God as an old man with a white beard. Suddenly, you see

God as mystery, and you realize that somehow you participate in that mystery."

When you enter into a religious conversion, you are basically saying, "Somehow, I, as a human person, am in relationship to this mystery of God and I believe that God exists." You begin to wonder: "How does this mystery touch me in my life? How does it come to me? How does it express itself to me? I have chosen to believe that this mystery reveals itself in my own experience, my own history. I begin to understand that the answers to this mystery can be found in religion."

As a Christian, you already learned that God entered into Israel's history. The Word became flesh and dwelt among us. God is a revealing God. God entered into our time as Jesus Christ. Your new understanding of yourself and the mystery of God constantly appears through everyday experiences. You come to understand that you are in relationship with this mystery, but it only makes sense to you in the context of being a Catholic Christian. You choose to embrace Christianity. You choose to live out your life as a Christian within the Catholic Church.

3. "The next stage in the conversion process is intellectual," Father Gatto explains. "You know who you are. You have entered into the mystery of God. You see yourself as a Catholic Christian. As part of your intellectual conversion, you continue to seek out meaning and truth. You study. You read. You involve yourself in a faith community. You pray. You reflect. You do everything you can to deepen your intellectual understanding."

4. This leads to the fourth stage, which is called the moral conversion. It propels you to act in accord with what you have come to believe.

"You seek the good," Father Gatto explains. "You seek to live in harmony with what you have discovered about the mystery of God. The seeking of the good is much bigger than you are, and sometimes it means that you put yourself second. If you don't have this kind of moral conversion, you live a life that is shallow and self-focused. Your actions and your judgments are not based upon the greater good, but on your own self-interest. Moral conversion helps you move away from self-interest and allows you to always seek the good — no matter how painful that is."

> **"Faith strips the mask from the world and reveals God in everything. It makes nothing impossible and renders meaningless such words as anxiety, danger, and fear, so that the believer goes through life calmly and peacefully, with profound joy."**
>
> **— VENERABLE CHARLES DE FOUCAULD**

The conversion process is not something that happens once in a lifetime. It is an ongoing process in which you can move through the stages, forward or backward, jumping from one stage to another as your understanding of yourself, the world, God, and other people grows and deepens. You can't force someone to enter into a conversion process. You can encourage someone. You can support that person. But you cannot pressure or coerce someone to seek a deeper level of spiritual maturity.

Getting Stuck in One Stage

Sometimes people never attain an adult level of faith. They get stuck in the adolescent transition and live out their lives in constant questioning and doubting. Some are afraid to look beneath the surface and choose to live at a shallow level of existence. Others begin the conversion process but become discouraged and stop searching. Sometimes, people want to believe, but without a strong inner experience of God, their desire is not strong enough to sustain a faith commitment.

The most dramatic example of this occurred in the years following the Second Vatican Council, when many people who had memorized every word of the Baltimore Catechism fell away from the Church because external practices, such as not eating meat on Friday, were changed. Their "faith" was not centered in a religious experience of God but in a set of rules, and when the rules changed, they felt as if their faith had dissolved.

"That happened to a priest friend of mine," recalls Msgr. Stanton. "After Vatican II, he began to question the divinity of Christ. He left the priesthood and lost his faith. He became an agnostic. He eventually married. His wife asked me one time why I was never affected by this. I told her that he always held the institution of the Church on a pedestal, and after Vatican II, it all collapsed for him."

Daniel Callahan was editor of *Commonweal* in 1968 when he simply stopped believing. "I don't know why some people believe and others don't," he says. "To me, there's no rational explanation. I long ago gave up the notion that some were just smarter than others — things don't break down that way."

For his wife, Sidney, who converted to Catholicism at age 20, Dan's loss of faith was devastating. "I felt totally betrayed," she admits. "It was horrible, but that's the way it was. I thought he would believe if he could, so I accepted it. I had to accept it: what else was there to do? I think we argued and it was very painful for a long period, but then we just stopped talking about it. I think there is pain on both sides if you change your beliefs or your thoughts about something."

It never weakened Sidney Callahan's faith, however. The worst part for her was trying to raise their children as Catholics alone. "I taught Sunday school for seven years. My major response to any struggle or any sort of problem is to try harder: I will overcome this."

It's never easy when a loved one loses faith. What's sometimes even more perplexing, however, is when family members and friends claim to believe but refuse to go to Mass. It's part of a growing trend toward spirituality without religion.

Chapter Notes

A recent survey confirmed that as many as 60 percent . . .: Mary Johnson, Dean R. Hoge, William Dinges, and Juan L. Gonzales, Jr., "Young Adult Catholics: Conservative? Alienated? Suspicious?" *America* (Vol. 180, No. 10; March 27, 1999).

"The death of our childhood faith makes us feel sick of heart . . .": Mark Link, S.J., *Path Through Catholicism* (Tabor Publishing, 1991).

"In faith, one does not see a different world . . .": Michael and Jana Novak, *Tell me Why* (Pocket Books, 1998).

"Just as we cannot force a plant to grow . . .": Henri J. M. Nouwen, *Reaching Out* (Doubleday and Co., 1975).

"It is a complete change of heart . . .": From the author's interview with Father Joseph Gatto.

"I don't know why some people believe and others don't . . .": Peter Occhiogrosso, *Once a Catholic* (Ballantine Books, 1987).

"I felt totally betrayed . . .": Ibid.

Chapter 8

Spiritual But Not Religious

—⸗—

"I was one of those who thought I was spiritual but didn't need religion. How wrong I was!" — R.G.

A Different Kind of Catholic

Greg Dolezal tries to touch base with his adult children every so often for an update on their faith lives. Sometimes, he doesn't know whether to be happy or sad.

"I find that they have kept the basic principles of the faith," he says, "but they seem to have lost contact with the practices."

When he asked his daughter how she felt about the Protestant church she visited recently, she told him, "It was strange." When he asked if she had considered changing religions, she told him in no uncertain terms, "Dad, I'm Catholic!"

"Yet she doesn't go to Mass very often," Greg observes. "I think it must be a very internal, value-oriented form of Catholicism that young people feel today. The rituals just don't mean as much."

A Private Matter?

Greg's experience with his adult children reflects a strange new trend toward spirituality that distances itself from organized religion. It's not uncommon to hear people of all ages say they still believe but have drifted away from the regular practice of the Catholic faith.

Steve Twomey says there wasn't anything in particular he disliked about the Catholic Church. "It retains a deep, primal grip on my innards," he admits. "But I've drifted like so many others. There was no dramatic break over Church position on those hot-button issues so often cited by lapsed Catholics. The Church didn't fail me because it was out of step. Religion just got to be too time-consuming. Building a career seemed more important. Dating seemed more important, particularly if you'd gone to my high school. The Church wasn't hip. It was the same every Sunday. What it had to offer — guidance, maybe some answers — didn't appear necessary because I was self-absorbed enough to think I was doing fine all by myself."

> **It's not uncommon to hear people of all ages say they still believe, but they have drifted away from the regular practice of the Catholic faith.**

Increasingly, people like Steve begin to see faith as a private matter between God and themselves. They see no need to go to church or take an active role in a faith community. They have reduced spirituality to individualism.

"I am Catholic, but I don't feel like I have to be in a church to worship God," explains a young woman from Kansas City. "I can worship God in church, outdoors, or at home equally well."

Decline in Church Attendance

Recent studies confirm that 96 percent of people in the United States believe in God, and 69 percent of Americans belong to a church. While these percentages have remained fairly stable over the past 40 years, the number of Americans who attend church regularly has declined to only 40 percent. Among Catholics, the percentages are slightly higher, with approximately 46 percent attending Mass weekly. But this number has dropped significantly from 1973, when 55 percent of Catholics attended Mass regularly, and 1963, when 71 percent were at church every Sunday.

In Canada, the situation is much worse. An Angus Reid poll commissioned by the *Toronto Globe and Mail* found that 84 percent of Canadians profess belief in God and 67 percent say religious faith is very important in their day-to-day life. However, only 20 percent of Canadians attend church weekly.

Canadian sociologist Reginald Bibby says most people aren't leaving their churches, they just aren't going to them.

This trend toward the personalization of religion is even more apparent among teenagers and young adults. In a recent survey, *Newsweek* magazine found that teenagers today talk about spirituality more, but they aren't always more religious. Seventy-eight percent said their religion was important to them, but only half said they attend services regularly, a figure that has declined significantly since the 1970s.

A similar survey conducted by *Seventeen* magazine found that 82 percent of the respondents considered themselves religious, but only 34 percent considered themselves "by the book" participants. Forty-eight percent said they followed religion on their own terms, picking and choosing what they wanted to believe, and not always attending traditional religious services.

Finding 'A Sense of Belonging' Elsewhere

Tom Beaudoin, author of *Virtual Faith: The Irreverent Spiritual Quest of Generation X*, says young people crave belonging and a sense of stability. "There's a real thirst for community, joy, and relationships that drives young people into thinking about spiritual life," he explains. But he also notes that coffeehouses and Internet chat rooms are taking the place of churches. "These places function as religious spaces, where young people are more likely to reveal themselves. The Internet allows teens an anonymity and an intimacy not always present at home or in church."

> **Tom Beaudoin notes that coffeehouses and Internet chat rooms are taking the place of churches.**

Researcher George Barna predicts that within the next 10 years "cyberchurches" on the Internet will claim as much as 10 to 20 percent of all organized religious activity.

"I was baptized Catholic and attended Catholic school, but I am not practicing and do not believe in organized religion," admits one young adult. "All Christian religions are too filled with contradictions. Having said all this, let me say that I am a spiritual person who believes in God and depends on God for guidance and protection. I live by faith (not religion). I pray. I have no reason to fear God. Religion entraps people's souls with dogma and fear. Faith sets the soul free to experience love and companionship with God."

Faith in Whom?

St. Augustine observed, however, that if you believe only what you like and you reject what you don't like, "it is not the Gospel you believe, but yourself."

When spirituality becomes self-centered, people begin to focus only on their own relationship with God and how it makes them feel. Once that happens, they find ways to justify why they don't go to Mass.

"The dictionary says that to worship is 'to feel extreme adoration or devotion,' " one woman insists. "The keyword is 'feel.' It's not where we worship that counts, but how we worship. What you feel becomes a part of you. It is reflected in your life. This kind of worship can be done at any time and in any place. You do not need a Mass or a priest to worship God."

Faith and Feelings

Father Leon Biernat, vocation director for the Diocese of Buffalo, disagrees. "Faith is not emotional," he says. "Faith is a consent of the will and knowledge of the mind and heart. Certainly we can feel good about religion at times, but if faith is reduced to an emotion or feeling, that is very shallow and it is not really faith."

Some of the greatest mystics in the Catholic tradition emphasize that real faith is often devoid of feelings. They called it a "dark night of the soul," when prayer, devotions, and liturgies seem dry, and there is a painful sense that God has somehow abandoned them. The purpose of this "dark night" is to strip them from reliance on warm feelings so that they can rely on faith alone. It's hard to imagine St. John of the Cross or St. Teresa of Ávila saying, "I don't feel anything in this monastery, so I'm not going to Mass anymore!" That is not what the Catholic tradition is about.

"The idea that everybody has their own private telephone line to God works against the communal spirit of the Catholic Church as 'People of God' who care about one another," explains Father John Catoir. "We have to help people overcome this distorted sense of individualism because it is not rich spirituality. We are not just individual souls. St. Teresa of Ávila talked about the soul as a house with many levels, but it is also a house on a block with many other houses in a city and in a country. The house is not an isolated place. There has to be a sense of community."

> **"If faith is scarce, it is because there is too much selfishness in the world, too much egoism. Faith, in order to be authentic, has to be generous and giving. Love and faith go hand in hand."**
>
> **— MOTHER TERESA OF CALCUTTA**

"A lot of people see religion and the Catholic Church as a list of restrictions and things you can't do," one teenager explains. "I tell my friends that it's more than that. All religions can be a source of love that can keep you on a good path through life and help you through the rough times."

Part of an Overall Trend

Syndicated columnist Father Ronald Rolheiser, O.M.I., believes the trend toward people who call themselves spiritual but not religious points to a breakdown of community at all levels of society. He suggests that people are treating their churches the same way they treat their families and their neighbors. "We want them to be there (when we need them), but we do not want them to make any regular or unconditional demands on us," he explains. "We pick, for our own purposes, what occasions we want to be present at, how much we will be involved, and for the rest we remain free and non-committed, guarding our own time and interests. Generally, we want them — extended family and neighborhood — to celebrate special occasions with, rites of passage, Christmas, Easter, Thanksgiving, and the like; but outside of that we want to be left alone. We reject any sense of obligation to them and resent any active interference or challenge they might bring into our lives."

Father Rolheiser believes that this concept of "pathological individualism" and "excessive sense of privacy" must be challenged. "Especially what must be challenged is the fallacy, as omnipresent as the air we breathe, that our lives are all our own, that we owe nothing to anyone beyond ourselves, and that we can buy into family and neighborhood how and when we feel like it," he insists.

"We were expected to attend Mass until we started college," one young adult explains. "I think children under age 18 should attend Mass with their parents."

Nurturing A Sense of Community

Father Gary Bagley, director of the youth department for the Diocese of Buffalo, believes it is the responsibility of families to nurture a strong sense of community by going to Mass together. Once young adults move away from home, they take on the responsibility for their own spiritual lives. But while children and teenagers are still living in the family, Father Bagley believes that going to Mass should be part of a family's weekly routine.

"There are some things we don't give teenagers a choice about," he says. "We don't ask kids if they want to go to the dentist. That's not a choice. Going to Mass with the family should not be a choice. A kid said to me one time, 'Do you think it's fair that my parents force me to go to Mass?' I said, 'No, absolutely not. It's not fair that they force you to eat their food. It's not fair that they force you to sleep in their house. It's not fair that they force you to go in their car when you want a ride to the mall. It's not fair that they make you go on vacation with them. They are really not fair.' "

This approach doesn't work if it creates anger, tension, and resentment, however. Families have to work hard to find meaning in going to Mass together.

Susan Reimer, a columnist for the Baltimore *Sun*, offers the following five suggestions that proved successful in encouraging her teenagers to attend Mass with the family:

1. **State your expectations and then stop talking.** "Getting up and out of the house on Sunday morning doesn't always go smoothly," she admits. "I try to state the departure time and then stop talking, refusing to be drawn into an . . . uh . . . discussion."

2. **Give them something to look forward to.** "It is an informal family ritual to go out for hamburgers after church," she says. "This meal is sacred to our busy family, one of the few the four of us can eat together."

3. **Make it relevant.** "Pray for hits" was her husband's whispered advice to her fidgeting son at Mass during baseball season.

4. **Act as if it doesn't matter to you.** When she told her teenage son that it was up to him as to whether he wanted to be confirmed, he joined the class with enthusiasm.

5. **Live it, and they will believe it. Preach it, and they will use it against you.** Teenagers are especially alert to hypocrisy. Faith has to be an integral part of family life, and that means making religion a family priority.

A Self-Exam

What kind of a witness are you to the Catholic faith?

"I teach religious education in my parish," one woman explains. "We have one hour a week with the kids. But I've found that many parents complain loudly that their kids are too stressed already with school, sports, music, and other activities to have any time left to give to religious education. Until parents' attitudes change, it's going to be an uphill battle."

Father Paul Nogaro, pastor of St. Stephen's Parish in Grand Island, N.Y., suggests that Catholics who are concerned about the faith lives of family members or friends must take a serious look at their own faith experience. He urges people to ask themselves whether they are joyful Catholics:

- Do you go to Mass?
- Do you get involved in your parish?
- Do you try to work with others to make the parish better?
- Do you reflect a deep sense of inner peace and joy that comes from your faith?

Or, Father Nogaro asks, are you a gloomy Catholic?

- Do you skip Mass frequently?
- Do you talk negatively about the Catholic Church or your parish?
- Do you refuse to get involved in parish events?
- Do you reflect a sense of anger, cynicism, distrust, or indifference toward the Church?

"If you're not excited about being Catholic, then you're not going to convince anyone else," Father Nogaro says. "People are attracted by those who have a joyful love of God and others."

Finding a New Parish

Sometimes, moving to another parish where everyone in the family can develop a sense of belonging will make a difference.

Msgr. William Stanton remembers the time a middle-aged couple, who were very active at another parish, came to see him. "They asked if they could join our parish because their kids didn't want to go to Mass at their own parish anymore," he recalls. "The parents loved the other parish, but the kids said it was boring. The kids wanted to come over to our parish because we had an active youth-ministry group and they had friends from school who were parishioners. I welcomed them into our parish, and the whole family became very active. One of their children was married in the parish several months ago. He still goes to Mass every week."

"Today, Christ asks the baptized: 'Are you my witnesses?' And each of us is invited to question sincerely: 'Do I offer the world the witness the Lord asks of me? Do I live a strong, serene and joyful faith? Or do I portray the image of a Christian life that is flagging, marred by compromises and easy conformity?' "

— POPE JOHN PAUL II

Before parents make a sacrifice like this, it's important for the whole family to sit down and talk. The parents might have to say to their kids, "What are you looking for?" The family may have to "shop" together for a parish. Msgr. Stanton suggests that when you search, you should look for a parish that has good liturgies. Look for a parish where the staff is open and welcoming. "Does the parish respond to the needs of the community?" he asks. "Do people work together to make the parish alive and vibrant? Parishes should have an impact on people's lives. That is what the Word and the liturgy are supposed to do."

Getting Involved

It's also important to look for a parish community where the whole family can become active and involved. It's not simply a matter of looking for the shortest Mass or the best homilies or the nicest music. "Being emotionally satisfied by a parish is part of it, but not all of it," Father Bagley warns. "We're seeing a lot of folks who are saying, 'What does this parish do for me?' But that is not the most important question. The essential religious question is: 'When I'm part of this parish, what does it help me to do for others?' As soon as you understand this distinction, the 'I don't get anything out of it' piece gets put into perspective. The parish should be a nurturing place, but that is only half of the equation. You should also look for a parish that challenges you to grow as individuals and as a family."

The understanding that real faith is a commitment to God and to others that is not based on "personal feelings" goes against the grain of a consumer-oriented society that seduces people into thinking that their own personal satisfaction brings happiness. When people of all ages begin to turn away from the Catholic Church because they don't "feel" anything, their quest for spiritual sustenance doesn't usually stop. The old saying that nature abhors a vacuum is true in the spiritual realm as well as the scientific. There are very few atheists in North America today. When a person begins to feel disconnected from the Catholic Church, they will almost always find some alternative. Sometimes, they pick and choose from a variety of different religions.

Chapter Notes

"It retains a deep, primal grip on my innards . . .": Steve Twomey, "Once a Catholic," *Catholic Digest* (April 1996).

Recent studies confirm that 96 percent of people in the United States believe in God, and 69 percent of Americans belong to a church . . .: George Gallup, Jr., and D. Michael Lindsay, *Surveying the Religious Landscape* (Morehouse Publishing, 1999).

An Angus Reid poll . . .: Charles Moore, "Faith in the Lives of Canadians: Most of Us Profess Faith in God, but Few Attend Church," *Western Catholic Reporter* (June 19, 2000).

Seventy-eight percent said their religion was important . . .: John Leland, "Searching for a Holy Spirit," *Newsweek* (May 8, 2000).

A similar survey conducted by Seventeen *magazine . . .:* Jana Siegal, "Keeping the Faith," *Seventeen* (July 2000).

"There's a real thirst for community, joy, and relationships . . .": Ibid.

Researcher George Barna predicts . . .: John Leland, "Searching for a Holy Spirit," *Newsweek* (May 8, 2000).

"We want them to be there . . .": Ron Rolheiser, O.M.I., "Why Fewer People Are Going to Church," *Western Catholic Reporter* (Nov. 23, 1998.

"Especially what must be challenged is the fallacy . . .": Ibid.

Susan Reimer, a columnist for the Baltimore Sun, *offers the following five suggestions . . .:* Susan Reimer, "My Son the Saint," *Catholic Digest* (November 1999).

Chapter 9

Dabbling in Other Faiths

"I would describe myself as an à la carte Catholic. I took a little bit of Catholicism and combined it with some other spiritualities." — R.W.

Customized Catholicism

When *Newsweek* magazine did a special report on teenagers today, 16-year-old Ashling Gabig, a student at a Catholic high school in Los Angeles, admitted that she has customized her Catholic beliefs to include personal prayer and karma. "My perceptions of God and religion are quite different from those of a devout Catholic," she says.

Ashling is not alone. There is an increasing trend among people of all ages to dabble in different Christian and non-Christian faiths. While churchgoing and allegiance to a particular religion declines, interest in spirituality is on the rise among all age groups.

The Search for Spiritual Growth

In their predictions for the future, George Gallup, Jr., and Timothy Jones expect that interest in "spiritual life" will continue to rise. "Measurably higher numbers say they want to grow spiritually," they report. "Interest in the 'spiritual life' has registered on indicator after indicator of cultural attention."

The actual percentage of Americans who say they feel a need to experience spiritual growth climbed 24 points in just four years – from 58 percent in 1994 to 82 percent in 1998. The percentage of Americans who say they have thought a lot about "the basic meaning and value of their lives" has risen 11 points, from 58 percent in 1985 to 69 percent today.

Father Ronald Rolheiser, O.M.I., describes the quest for spirituality as "an unquenchable fire, a restlessness, a longing, a disquiet, a hunger, a loneliness, a gnawing nostalgia, a wildness that cannot be tamed, a congenital all-embracing ache that lies at the center of human experience and is the ultimate force that drives everything else."

In looking at the past, Catholics can trace a long history of holy men and women who embarked on a spiritual quest within the framework of the Catholic Church. They transformed their own lives and the lives of others. They experimented with different prayer forms. They reformed existing religious communities or founded new ones. But their efforts were all focused within the structure of Catholic tradition and the Gospel message.

The New Age Movement

Today, spiritual seekers often end up with an eclectic spirituality of their own. It's not hard to find Catholics, for instance, who have incorporated New Age beliefs in reincarnation, astrology, spiritualism, channeling, animism, fortune-telling, and even witchcraft into their belief systems.

"In the New Age phenomenon, there is a tremendous flurry of activity, teaching, lectures, and tapes to help people find their way to a spiritual life or consciousness where they will be above their fears," explains syndicated columnist Father John Catoir. "Very often, the New Agers are introduced to a form of mysticism, which basically is a turning into self through meditation or trance or an altered state of consciousness."

"My spirituality is a meld of many things, some of which I would attribute to what the Catholic Church has taught me, some from things I have learned from other faiths, and some that I have discovered myself along the way," one young adult admits. "Some people feel this is a bad thing and not being true to my religion. I do not view it as such. I am very comfortable with it."

Fundamentalism

On the opposite extreme, there are Catholics who attend Fundamentalist Bible studies and prayer services. When asked in a recent Gallup Poll whether they would describe themselves as "born again," or "Evangelical," Christians, 21 percent of Catholics said yes, a significant increase from the 12 percent who described themselves as born again, or Evangelical, in 1988.

"We have quite a few Catholic families who go to both churches," explains a former Catholic who now belongs to a Fundamentalist church. "They go to Mass on Saturday night, and to our church on Sunday morning. They attend our Sunday schools and Bible studies for adults and children."

Religion Cafeteria-style

Canadian sociologist Reginald Bibby calls this phenomenon "religion à la carte."

In their recent study of religious practices in the United States today, George Gallup, Jr., and D. Michael Lindsay confirm that this growing interest in spirituality has resulted in a complex jumble of attitudes and behaviors, not just among Catholics but in all religious denominations. They have observed:

- "The glaring lack of knowledge about the Bible, basic doctrines, and the traditions of one's church."
- "The inconsistencies of belief — for example, Evangelical Christians expressing belief in New Age practices."
- "The superficiality of faith, with many people not knowing what they believe, or why."
- "A belief in God, but a lack of trust in God."
- "A failure on the part of organized religion in some respects to make a profound difference in our society, despite the fact that churches reach six out of 10 Americans in a given month."

Some Possible Reasons

1. **Our multicultural society:** Some say this eclectic mix of religious beliefs stems from our increasingly multicultural society. People today are exposed to religions and spiritual movements that previous generations never encountered. Catholics find themselves drawn by people from other faith traditions into faith-sharing groups, discussions, lectures, prayer meetings, Bible studies, and casual conversations at school, in the workplace, and in the neighborhood.

   "When you're young and single, you often feel like you have no place in the Catholic Church," a young adult explains. "People in non-denominational churches

Catholics: A Statistical Overview

Almost one out of four (24 percent) American adults attends a Catholic church. In 1999, researcher George Barna compiled the following statistical profile of Catholics based on recent national surveys:

Income
- 25 percent earn $25,000 or less annually.
- 40 percent earn between $25,000 and $50,000.
- 36 percent earn over $50,000 each year.

Marital Status
- 58 percent of Catholics are married.
- 42 percent of Catholics are single.
- 21 percent of Catholics are currently divorced or have been divorced in the past.

Ethnicity
- 70 percent are white.
- 25 percent are Hispanic.
- 2 percent are African-American.

Education
- 35 percent have a high school degree or less.
- 32 percent took college courses but did not graduate.
- 32 percent are college graduates or have advanced degrees.

Faith Commitment
- 47 percent attend Mass weekly.
- 41 percent say they are absolutely committed to the Christian faith.
- 18 percent read the Bible within the past week (not including when at Mass).
- 11 percent are committed to sharing their faith with others.

are friendly, and they invite you to Bible study for single people and dynamic singles ministries where you can meet other young adults. Catholics just go to Mass and it's easy to be completely anonymous."

2. **Technology:** Advances in technology have created a global society. While Catholics of previous generations would rely on Sunday sermons for guidelines on what Catholics believe, today you can learn not just about your own religion but also facts and faith foundations about almost every other religion in the world through the media and the Internet. Websites such as *Beliefnet.com* offer a smorgasbord of faith traditions, with the opportunity to develop a virtual sense of community through online discussion in chat rooms.

3. **Interfaith marriage:** The blending of religious beliefs in interfaith marriages has also had a tremendous impact on families. A 14-year-old from Michigan is a prime example. The daughter of a Catholic mother and a Jewish stepfather, she did not practice either faith while she was growing up. She started attending Baptist services with friends, but she also has friends in a Jewish youth group. Her mother recently returned to the Catholic Church, so the teen has started to go to Mass on Sundays. But she still holds a very Fundamentalist view of Scripture.

4. **Cultural counter-messages:** Secularism and materialism send strong counter-messages about what is important in life. Many Catholics no longer understand or accept the moral teachings of the Church. As the fabric of society disintegrates, family life erodes. A "lukewarm" faith does not sustain them.

Many have never felt an inner experience of God's presence.

5. **Watered-down religious education:** Some people blame what they call a watering-down of Catholic religious education in the past 30 years that left a whole generation without a firm faith foundation upon which they can deepen their relationship with God, with the Church, and with other people. "I did not take ownership of my spiritual growth," a middle-aged man confessed. "You get out of church just what you put into it. I invested nothing, and I got nothing in return. I went through the motions of going, but I really never invested any serious time or commitment to it."

Looking for Something 'New'

It's not uncommon for Catholics to admit that what they know about their faith seems old and stale. They are look-

What Catholics Say They Believe

When asked in a recent survey whether Catholics should follow the teachings of the pope and "not take it upon themselves to decide differently," only 25 percent of the Catholics surveyed agreed. In the same survey, only 9 percent of Catholics considered birth control wrong for married couples; about half (48 percent) considered premarital sex to be always wrong; 58 percent thought abortion is always wrong no matter what the circumstances; 52 percent favored capital punishment.

ing for something new and exciting. What they don't realize is that everything they desire is already present in the Catholic Church.

"My sister is a feminist and she sees the Catholic Church in terms of oppression," one woman admits. "She has a very limited understanding of Catholicism. She doesn't know about the brilliant women who have been Catholic. I send her books on women like Dorothy Day and Edith Stein so she can see that there's more to being a Catholic woman than just having babies."

Reaching Out

These kinds of personal efforts to reach out to friends or family members who are dabbling in other faith traditions can make a difference. In November 1999, the American bishops issued a document entitled "Our Hearts Were Burning Within Us," which provides a pastoral plan for adult faith formation that is designed to help adults strengthen their faith so they can, in turn, reach out to others. The bishops are asking dioceses and parishes to meet the needs and interests of adults by offering actual life experiences and diverse adult programs that will include Scripture study and the teaching of the Church's tradition in a variety of vibrant learning environments.

"We move ahead full of hope, knowing this vision of adult faith formation can become reality," the bishops wrote. "Jesus the Risen One is still with us, meeting us on the pathways of our lives, sharing our concerns, enlightening us with his word, strengthening us with his presence, nourishing us in the breaking of the bread, and sending us forth to be his witnesses. In the providence of God the Father, the action of the Holy Spirit will rekindle the fire of love in the hearts of the faithful and renew the catechetical dynamism of the Church. Awakened and energized by the Spirit, let us strengthen our commitment and intensify our efforts to help the adults in our communities be touched and transformed by the life-giving message of Jesus, to explore its meaning, experience its power, and live in its light as faithful adult disciples today. Let us do our part with creativity and vigor, our hearts aflame with love to empower adults to know and live the message of Jesus. This is the Lord's work. In the power of the Spirit it will not fail but will bear lasting fruit for the life of the world."

> **"I believe some people — lots of people — pray through the witness of their lives, through the work they do, the friendships they have, the love they offer people and receive from people."**
>
> **— DOROTHY DAY**

Drawing Catholics Back to Their Roots

As new avenues for Catholic information and evangelization open, it is very likely that the quest for spiritual truth will draw Catholics back to their roots. Some say it's starting to happen already.

- "I came back to the Catholic Church after seeing what New Age was really about," one woman admits. "It promises healing and fulfillment, but everything had a price tag. I began to feel as if evil was entering my life. I saw only emptiness before me. I realized now how far away from God I had wandered. I was afraid that God had abandoned me, but the Catholic Church welcomed me back with open arms.

- "I am a 28-year-old cradle Catholic," a young man says. "I went along my merry way rejecting everything I was taught until I reached the point where I felt like I needed answers. I went searching for them. I believed with all my heart that God wanted me to know him more and love him more. I needed to know the hows and whys. I was searching and I found a huge fountain of resources out in other religions. By accident one day, I found a Catholic website and I discovered how much Catholicism fits Scripture. Now instead of going through the motions with other religions, I have found love and truth in going to Mass. Going to Communion is so much more for me that my knees tremble when walking up to receive the Body and Blood of Christ. I discovered that the answers are right here in the Catholic Church."

Not everyone comes to the same conclusion, however.

Chapter Notes

"My perceptions of God and religion . . .": John Leland, "Searching for a Holy Spirit," *Newsweek* (May 8, 2000).

"Measurably higher numbers say they want to grow spiritually . . .": George Gallup, Jr., and Timothy Jones, *The Next American Spirituality: Finding God in the Twenty-first Century* (Cook Communications Ministries, 2000).

The actual percentage of Americans who say they feel . . .: George Gallup, Jr., and D. Michael Lindsay, *Surveying the Religious Landscape* (Morehouse Publishing, 1999).

". . . *an unquenchable fire, a restlessness, a longing, a disquiet, a hunger . . .*": Ronald Rolheiser, *The Holy Longing* (Doubleday, 1999).

When asked in a recent Gallup Poll whether they would describe themselves . . .": *Surveying the Religious Landscape.*

"*In their recent study of religious practices . . .*": Ibid.

"*We move ahead full of hope, knowing this vision . . .*": "Our Hearts Were Burning Within Us: A Pastoral Plan for Adult Faith Formation in the United States," NCCB/USCC (Nov. 17, 1999).

Sidebar: *Catholics: A Statistical Overview*: George Barna, Barna Research Ltd.

Sidebar: *What Catholics Say They Believe*: Thomas P. Sweetster, S.J., "The Parish: What Has Changed, What Remains?" *America* (Feb. 17, 1996).

Chapter 10

Leaving the Catholic Church

"I converted to Lutheranism. It has been a tremendous learning experience, and I will never regret this part of my spiritual journey." — M.J.

Converts to Another Christian Denomination

After years of experience in working with people who feel alienated from the Catholic Church, Msgr. William Gallagher has developed a theory. "Fallen-away Catholics haven't really left," he explains. "They are still Catholics, and they still identify themselves as such even if they don't go to Mass. They are a much easier group to deal with because they have retained their Catholic roots. Many of them eventually return to the Catholic Church. It's a different story when family members or friends convert to another religion."

Pat and Chuck Kramer fit into the second category. Before they were married, Chuck converted to Catholicism. Every Sunday, they went to their local parish for Mass. "Chuck was getting nothing out of it," Pat recalls. "We probably should have tried another parish, but I was raised in the old school — that you go where you are located geographically."

When they moved to a new town, they joined the local parish, which turned out to be even worse than the one they had left. There was no sense of community, the Masses

did not inspire them, and the pastor had a very conde-
scending attitude. They continued to go to Mass every
Sunday – even during football season when they had season tickets and had to rush from Mass to the stadium.

One Sunday, during the homily, the priest announced,
"I'm sick and tired of people coming to Mass dressed for
football games!"

"That was the icing on the cake," Pat recalls. "There
were several things that this priest said that Chuck did not
agree with, but after that Sunday, Chuck said, 'I will never
go back there again.' I had to do some soul-searching, and
I admitted that I was not all that happy in the Catholic
Church either."

Spiritual Growth

They eventually ended up in the Wesleyan Church, which
Pat believes has offered "a spiritual depth" that they never
found in the Catholic Church. "The spiritual growth here
is so much greater," she says. "They teach from the Bible,
and the church is just blossoming."

Pat feels that she has found truth in the Wesleyan
Church. "I have found spiritual growth, truth, and consis-
tency," she says. "People are actually living what Jesus
taught and struggling to do it. They are struggling, but
they are teachable. They are willing to work at it. They are
willing to go to Bible study. They are willing to read. They
are willing to do what they have to do to search for truth."

She calls the Wesleyan Church an "equipping" church.
"It helps you to deal with your problems, and it equips
you to help other people deal with their problems," she
explains. "I feel that this is what the early Church was all

about. We have a lot of self-help groups. We have divorce care, a diet workshop that is biblically based, a cancer-care support group, Alcoholics Anonymous, and other dependency groups. On Sunday, we have Bible study and how the Bible relates to everyday life. There are parenting classes that teach unconditional love for your children, as Jesus has unconditional love for you. Our church is very balanced. I feel as if I've grown a lot. I believe the Lord has called me to go here because I have peace about it. Each person has to go where they are called."

Switching Denominations

Pat predicts that it will be easier for the next generation of Catholics to switch churches. Studies show that she may be right. Within recent years, there has been a growing trend among American Protestants to switch denominations. Nearly one adult in four (23 percent) has moved at least once from the religious group in which he or she was raised. If religious loyalty to a particular Protestant denomination is eroding, what does that mean for Catholics?

Nearly one adult in four has moved at least once from the religious group in which he or she was raised.

Catholic Identity

Increasingly, concerns about the strength of Catholic identity have been raised. A recent poll shows that 45 percent of American Catholics describe their faith as "not strong." Thirty-six percent of Catholics said their faith is less important to them than it was to their parents. Younger Catholics are twice as likely to say their faith is less important to them than it was for their parents' generation.

While studies show that most young Catholics who drift away eventually turn back to religion, only 86 percent return to the practice of the Catholic faith. The other 14 percent join other churches or synagogues.

"I didn't understand a lot of Catholic rituals because I suppose I was never really educated," admits a former Catholic who joined a non-denominational church. "Everything in the Catholic Church was so formal, so traditional. I was sitting in church watching people say the same things over and over with no meaning. They were just reciting words. I saw them receive the Eucharist and then sit down and talk about others. I heard more people talk about what others were wearing than being excited about being with the Lord. Why would I want this? So I went somewhere where I was not only embraced by the church body, but by God's Word and his love."

Finding God Elsewhere?

Msgr. William Stanton admits that if years ago he heard about someone who had converted to another faith, he would have automatically said, "Isn't that awful?" But today he takes a different approach. "I would want to know about the maturity of the person who left," he says. "Was that person happy when he or she was Catholic? Were they dissatisfied with the Catholic Church? Was there something missing in their relationship with God? Did they find a relationship with the Lord that is more personal than what they had before? Was the opportunity for that kind of relationship never presented to them in the Catholic Church? Are they happy now? Are they trying to live a good life?"

If the answers to those questions are yes, you have to at least consider the possibility that maybe this person was drawn into this other religion for a reason:

- "I found God in another church," one man explains. "All I had to do is ask Jesus to come into my heart. I read the Bible every day. We sing and clap in church. We pray to God through Jesus with no in-betweens. I have been set free from drugs, alcohol, and cigarettes. I am so happy with my life."

- "Some family members and friends were astonished when I left the Catholic Church," another woman admits. "I was ridiculed a bit, but I didn't let it bother me. I am having an incredible relationship with Our Lord. I can honestly turn the other cheek when people make fun of me or say I'm wrong for leaving the Catholic Church. I love Our Lord! I am different because of his love. I have peace. I have a sound mind. I accept responsibility for my own actions and don't blame others. I have a wonderful, godly man for a husband and wonderful, loving children. I have so much more — and I'm not talking about material things or money. I'm talking about spiritual richness. If some family members cannot accept this, then I'm sorry. I try not to create conflict. It's not that I don't like Catholics or that I'm against the religion, but I am at a place in my life where I need to grow as a Christian. I am not trying to convert people or get people away from the Catholic faith. I respect other people's point of view and show them how God has affected my life by allowing them to see the change in me. What else can I do except pray and continue to be there for them if they need me?"

Keep in mind that a spiritual journey may take twists and turns that are beneficial to the traveler. Some of those turns may involve a time away from the Catholic Church in order to understand better all that the Church possesses and passes on to its members.

"My grandfather gave me his blessing and told me he thought I wouldn't really be Catholic until I left and saw what I was missing," one woman admits. "The road back for me actually began when I had a miscarriage. I was appalled by the trite comments I was subjected to at my Protestant church. Up until that point, I thought they were as pro-life as I was, just a little weak on the seamless-garment doctrine. That was when I realized I would be more at home in the Catholic Church. Also, I have a background in history and philosophy. I'm used to hearing about the Church Fathers and missed that terribly in Lutheranism. I just felt this big void there that had been filled by the grandness of Catholic tradition. I missed it."

> "Don't give in to discouragement. No more must you do so when you try to settle a marriage crisis or convert a sinner and don't succeed. If you are discouraged, it is a sign of pride because it shows you trust in your own powers. . . . Leave it to Jesus."
>
> — **MOTHER TERESA OF CALCUTTA**

God's Ways Are Not Ours

God works in strange and mysterious ways. Sometimes people come back to the Church. Sometimes they don't. They may be drawn into another religion for a reason that is beyond our understanding. As part of this process, maybe you are being called to let the person go:

- "We've had some hard feelings in my family concerning a little girl that my mother and I raised," explains a man from California. "After much discussion, we both felt that it was better for her to have involvement in another faith than to be unhappy in ours."
- "Four out of my five children have left the Catholic Church, but they are very religious," explains a woman from the Midwest. "I am disappointed that they left the Church, but I am not disappointed in them or in their relationship with the Lord. Actually, my daughter, who remained Catholic, could use some of what her brothers and sisters have found."

"Everyone has his or her own conscience," Msgr. Stanton points out. "We all have to live with the choices that we make."

The *Catechism of the Catholic Church* states: "Man has the right to act in conscience and in freedom so as personally to make moral decisions. He must not be forced to act contrary to his conscience. Nor must he be prevented from acting according to his conscience, especially in religious matters."

Canon law states, "All persons are bound to seek the truth in matters concerning God and God's Church; by divine law they are also obligated and have the right to embrace and to observe the truth which they have recognized. Persons cannot ever be forced by anyone to embrace the Catholic faith."

Following One's Conscience

When Stephen Dubner decided to reject Catholicism and embrace Judaism, he went to the late Cardinal John J. O'Connor of New York for advice on how to deal with his mother. She had converted to Catholicism from Judaism many years before. She could not accept her son's decision to practice the Jewish faith.

During a taped interview, Stephen Dubner told Cardinal O'Connor, "The greatest conflict between my mother and myself is that she sees Catholicism as the one true faith and Judaism as a once-valid religion that was necessarily superseded by Christianity. I don't mean to turn this into a shrink session, or a confessional, but how would you suggest that we go about resolving this conflict?"

Cardinal O'Connor suggested that he approach the situation in two ways. He advised him to begin by looking at recent declarations of Pope John Paul II about the validity of Judaism. Then he encouraged him to look at the teachings of the Second Vatican Council regarding the primacy of an informed conscience, which has resulted from thinking, discussion, reading, study, and prayer.

"Then," the cardinal concluded, "the deliberate decision that, okay, I know Catholicism, or I know this faith or I know that faith. I know what the Church teaches, I have studied it respectfully, I know what the papal encyclicals say, I have prayed over it, and I am convinced in conscience that God wants me to be this or to be that, to be Jewish, to be Lutheran, whatever it is. So . . . tell your mother that you have tried to study this, that you have prayed about it, this is not just a revolt or a rejection, this is not a dismissal of what you don't understand — that this is where you think God wants you to be, an informed Jew."

It wasn't until later that evening, when Stephen Dubner transcribed the interview tape, that he understood what Cardinal O'Connor was saying. He also understood the depths of his mother's pain. He knew how difficult it was for her to understand his point of view.

"I read over the cardinal's words on the validity of Judaism," he later recalled. "This would jolt her, I knew. And what about the informed conscience: Would she accept that? Did I accept that? Though I had studied a good bit about Christianity by now, I had hardly read every word of Church doctrine. But where did my allegiance lie? According to Jewish law, I was a Jew. Had my conscience, as a Jew, been informed by thinking, by discussion, by study, by prayer? Was I convinced in conscience that God wanted me to be a Jew? I was. I truly was."

An Authentic Conversion

In his study of the conversion process, Albert I. Gordon would call this kind of conversion "authentic" because it stems from reasons that are purely intrinsic, with no ulterior motives. "This type of convert is concerned only with finding what, to him, is the 'true' religion," Gordon says. "He is determined to worship God and to serve Him with the fullness of his heart, mind, and soul. The test I have used in all instances is a simple one: Has this convert *any other* motive for conversion than the desire to find the true God and serve Him to the best of his ability?"

Gordon also identifies two other types of converts:

- The *pro forma* convert is someone with no spiritual or deep personal reasons for conversion. This person's motives are often connected to the desire to marry someone who has a strong faith in a different religion. This kind of convert will meet all the requirements of conversion. "He is to be compared to the college student who has registered for a course in which he has not the slightest interest but which, once passed, will provide him with the college credits he needs for graduation," Gordon explains. "He may pass the course with a high mark and yet acquire absolutely nothing from all that he has studied simply because he has no real interest in or concern with it."

  The *pro forma* convert agrees to all the stipulations, meets all the requirements, and follows all the procedures, with one basic exception: The person's heart is not in it. He or she is a convert in name only.

- A second type of convert Gordon identifies is one who goes through the formal process of changing religions, but never really lets go of his or her original faith. Gordon calls these folks **marginal** converts because they live on the edge in a desperate attempt to maintain ties with both religions. "He lives in two worlds," Gordon explains, "with two religious philosophies whenever possible and is not completely 'at home' in either."

  The *pro forma* convert and the marginal convert are more likely to revert to their original faith if the circumstances in their lives change. They are most often found in interfaith marriages. In the next chapter, we'll take a closer look at interfaith marriage and the impact these kinds of marriages have on family members and friends.

Chapter Notes

Nearly one adult in four . . .: George Gallup, Jr., and D. Michael Lindsay, *Surveying the Religious Landscape* (Morehouse Publishing, 1999).

A recent poll shows that 45 percent of American Catholics . . .: Ibid.

While studies show that most young Catholics who drift away . . .: Mary Johnson, Dean R. Hoge, William Dinges, and Juan L. Gonzales, Jr., "Young Adult Catholics: Conservative? Alienated? Suspicious?" *America* (Vol. 180, No. 10; March 27, 1999).

"Man has the right to act in conscience . . .": *Catechism of the Catholic Church*, no. 1782.

"All persons are bound to seek the truth . . .": Code of Canon Law, Canon 748.

"The greatest conflict between my mother and myself . . .": Stephen J. Dubner, *Turbulent Souls* (Avon Books, 1998).

"This type of convert is concerned only with finding . . .": Albert I. Gordon, *The Nature of Conversion* (Beacon Press, 1967).

Chapter 11

Interfaith Marriage

"I was very upset when our son told us that he was getting married in a Protestant church and they did not plan to raise the children as Catholics. It was very hard to accept." — M.W.

The No. 1 Reason

Most people are surprised to learn that interfaith marriage is the No. 1 cause of someone leaving the Catholic faith. Studies show that in 1957, interfaith marriages accounted for only 6 percent of all weddings. Today, nearly 50 percent of all Catholics marry a person from another religion, and the percentage is usually much higher in areas where there are fewer Catholics. In about half of all interfaith marriages, one person converts to the other person's religion.

Sometimes, the spouse converts to Catholicism, and for the Catholic side of the family that is usually cause for celebration. But it doesn't always work out that way. When a couple intermarries, they face five possible options:

- He converts to her religion.
- She converts to his religion.
- They both retain their own faith.
- They compromise and both convert to a third religion.
- Or they decide to do nothing and practice no religion at all.

At St. James Parish in Jamestown, N.Y., four out of five weddings are what Catholics would call "mixed marriages."

"The population of Jamestown is about 18 percent Catholic," explains Msgr. Tony Attea, the pastor. "So the number of interfaith marriages is exactly according to proportion. A Catholic in Jamestown has a one-in-five chance of marrying another Catholic."

Gains and Losses

In practical terms, what that means is the parish tends to get a lot of new converts to Catholicism from other faiths, but it also loses a significant number of Catholics. "They don't always convert to the other faith," Msgr. Attea points out, "but they no longer come to Mass. Some of them end up going to Protestant churches. It depends on whose faith is stronger. I find that is true especially with men. They will stop coming to Mass and start to worship with their wives to keep them happy. I don't argue with that because I feel that the marriage bond is very important and I'm not going to be the judge. I'll leave it in the hands of God."

Social status also has an impact on which person converts. It is much more likely for a Catholic man or woman to convert if his or her spouse is more affluent or holds a higher position in the business or professional world.

"When I married a few years ago, it was to a Protestant," explains a young woman. "There was absolutely no chance of him converting to Catholicism, and I was unequipped to really sell Catholicism to him. It was my desire to be active in church, and so we decided on a Lutheran church that was quite similar to Catholicism."

It is becoming increasingly common, however, for couples in interfaith marriages to continue practicing their own faith. The richness of religious or cultural differences seems to add to the couple's attraction to each other. Msgr. Attea has a number of parishioners in this situation. "In some cases, the husband brings the wife to church, then he goes to his own church," Msgr. Attea explains. "Afterward, he picks her up and they go to breakfast. It seems to work as long as they respect each other's faith."

Premarital Preparation

When preparing couples for interfaith marriages, Msgr. Attea encourages them to learn as much as they can about the other person's religion. "If you have questions, you should ask them now," he warns.

He explains that Catholics consider marriage a sacrament. "You are united in the flesh, but you are also united in spirit," he tells them. "Every time you express your love to each other and consummate your relationship, you receive the grace of the sacrament."

During his 1982 trip to Great Britain, Pope John Paul II recognized the great number of interfaith marriages in that country. "To these families I say: You live in your marriage the hopes and difficulties of the path to Christian unity. Express that hope in prayer together, in the unity of love. Together invite the Holy Spirit of Love into your hearts and into your homes. The Holy Spirit will help you to grow in trust and understanding."

He encourages them to talk about how they will raise their children. He makes sure they both understand that according to Church law, the Catholic party has an obligation to do everything in his or her power to raise the children in the Catholic faith, although the Church does not hold the person responsible if it is not possible.

"If the Catholic is very strong in faith, the child will be raised Catholic — especially if the child understands the promise the mother or father made," Msgr. Attea says. "I've seen some very strong Catholic kids who were raised in mixed-religion marriages with both parents going to their own churches. But if the Catholic parent is not strong in his or her faith, the child will follow the faith of the more authentic parent. Kids are quick to see hypocrisy. If one parent is a Catholic and never goes to Mass, but the other parent is a Protestant and goes to church every Sunday, chances are the child is going to be a Protestant or nothing at all."

"My brother thinks church is for women because he never saw my dad go," one woman admits.

A Recent Study

In a recent study of interfaith marriages and same-faith marriages, Michael Lawler, a theology professor at Creighton University and director of the university's Center for Marriage and Family, found three predictors of marital stability:

1. The first emphasized the importance of joint involvement in religious activities.
2. The second indicated that the fewer religious differences a couple faced, the less likely that the marriage would end in divorce.

3. The third predictor, and the most significant, involved whether the extended family approved of the marriage.

Difficult Questions

"It's not easy when one of your kids decides to marry someone of another faith," a mother confesses. "You may like this person very much, but you know from your own experience how difficult marriage can be. The prospect of a mixed marriage raises a whole range of questions that you're afraid to ask because you don't want to seem like you're interfering. A part of you wants to be happy for your child, but another part of you is filled with all of these questions."

Some of the questions in the mind of a parent might include:

*   Where are they going to get married?
*   What religion will they choose?
*   In what religion will my grandchildren be raised?
*   How will this affect other family members?
*   How will this affect family traditions and holiday celebrations?

The worst part is that there might not be immediate answers to your questions or concerns. You may have to live with this for a while to see how it unfolds. You can certainly express some of your concerns in a way that is as non-threatening as possible, but it must always be done in an atmosphere of unconditional love. Ultimately, you must accept the fact that the decisions are not yours to make and that you will have to find some peaceful way to live with the outcome.

"My mother-in-law never tried to convert me," one woman recalled. "She was just a kind, accepting, hospitable woman who never offered unwanted advice. She knew how to accept a new Protestant daughter-in-law with a ready-made grandson. I expected to be greeted with dismay, but there was never even an objection to our marrying outside the Catholic Church. I'm willing to bet, however, that she was praying her Rosaries for us. God answered her prayers, and before she died she saw me converted to the Church, our marriage sacramentally blessed, and her little granddaughters receive their First Communion."

Non-Christian Interfaith Marriage

Many families find that the prospect of a marriage in certain religions is much more troubling than it is in others. It is particularly upsetting for many families when someone marries a non-Christian. According to the National Jewish Population Study, 31 percent of Christian spouses in intermarriage convert to Judaism, compared with 3 percent of Jewish spouses who convert to Christianity.

"Many couples try to resolve their differences by establishing what we call a bi-holiday home," explain Paul and Rachel Cowan, authors of *Mixed Blessings*. "They don't want to decide on one religion for the children, either because they are each genuinely fond of both traditions or because one parent is unwilling to let the other dominate in this important area. They balance the two by celebrating the four most familiar holidays — by lighting the Menorah, decorating the Christmas tree, having a seder, and hiding Easter eggs. They embellish these activities with special family traditions. They create wonderful celebrations. But these celebrations are just a glimpse of the fabrics of both religions. They don't teach much about Judaism or Christianity, or about identity and community."

Practicing No Religion

While the prospect of interfaith marriage can be stressful, most families find it especially troubling when a young couple decides to do nothing. At first, it might not seem like too much of a problem if they don't go to church. The couple might brush off any concerns about religion with the attitude, "It doesn't matter. Neither one of us is religious." It's another matter when they don't have their children baptized and the children are raised with no spiritual foundation.

Many young adults do return to the practice of some faith when their children start to ask questions about the meaning of life.

"It was very difficult for my parents when we decided not to have our children baptized," admits one young father. "My parents believe that you have to be baptized to get into heaven. But we didn't want to be hypocrites about it. If that's not what we believe, how could we agree to go through the motions?"

"All I can say is 'Pray for them,' " Msgr. Attea advises, "and hope they are in goodwill. When they miss their First Communions and confirmations and being part of the Catholic faith, maybe they will rethink their decision."

Many young adults do return to the practice of some faith when their children start to ask questions about the meaning of life.

Religion Is Not a Weapon

"I am a Catholic married to a non-Catholic," one woman explains. "My husband and I try to find spiritual harmony. We try not to be territorial about our beliefs. We try to see God in everyone. This allows us to avoid using religion as a weapon."

It's also important for extended family members and friends to avoid using religion as a weapon against couples in interfaith marriages — especially in cases where the Catholic has converted to another faith.

"My parents never came to see my kids baptized," explains a former Catholic who converted to a Protestant faith. "My oldest daughter is getting married this spring, and I don't know if my parents will come to the wedding. They still think it is a sin to go to a Protestant church. Some of my relatives say that I'm really messed up because I left the Catholic Church. Only one of my aunts stands up for me and says, 'Leave her alone. She's happy where she is.'"

Respecting Someone Else's Beliefs

It is important to try to respect another person's religious beliefs, even if you don't agree with them. The time may come when your son or daughter may need your help, but they will only accept it if they know that you respect them. "I returned to the Catholic faith because my husband became abusive," one woman admits. "My mother encouraged me to speak with a Protestant minister, and having had some bad experiences with Protestant ministers not respecting confidential matters, I refused. My mom realized that I needed a priest, and she called one for me. I always knew I was loved, even when I left the Church. And I was loved back in, by my family and a priest with kid gloves."

"The bottom line is always to love," says moral theologian Msgr. Angelo Caligiuri. "This is the Lord's approach. He didn't turn anyone away. He took them in and loved them into life."

It's Not Always Easy

A loving approach is especially difficult when a Catholic marries someone who belongs to a church where proselytizing is a major force. For example, some Fundamentalist and Pentecostal groups do not believe that Catholics are Christian, and as a result, they are convinced that Catholics will go to hell. They feel a responsibility to try to convert Catholics to what they believe is the truth.

One day a man complained to a rabbi about his son who had fallen away from the observance of the Jewish law. "What shall I do?" the man asked. "Do you love your son?" the rabbi said. "Of course I do," the man insisted. "Then love him even more," the rabbi advised.

"My brother's fiancée told me that Catholicism is a cult," a teenager reported. "She keeps trying to show me the differences between a Catholic Bible and a 'regular' Bible. She is very bothered about saints and Mary. My brother still goes to Mass on Saturday afternoon, but on Sunday morning he goes to her church. She told me she is going to save my brother and then she is going to save our whole family."

Increasing numbers of Catholic families face this problem. In the next chapter, we'll take a look at how to deal with loved ones who don't believe that Catholics are "saved."

Chapter Notes

Studies show that in 1957, interfaith marriages accounted for . . .: John Leland, "Searching for a Holy Spirit," *Newsweek* (May 8, 2000).

In a recent study of interfaith marriages . . .": "Religion Good for Marriage, Researcher says," News Briefs, Catholic News Service (March 21, 2000).

According to the National Jewish Population Study . . .: Judy Petsonk and Jim Remsen, *The Intermarriage Handbook: A Guide for Jews and Christians* (Quill/William Morrow, 1988).

"Many couples try to resolve their differences . . .": Paul Cowan and Rachel Cowan, *Mixed Blessings* (Doubleday, 1987).

Chapter 12

Encountering Fundamentalists

= =

"My sister left the Church about 15 years ago. This caused me a lot of pain. She joined a non-denominational church which is anti-Catholic. She feels the need to 'save' me from Catholicism now. It hurts because we can no longer share our religious views. We got into so many arguments that now I go out of my way to avoid religious topics altogether." — C.L.E.

Targeting Catholics

The pastor of a large Catholic parish in a small Midwestern town tells how a small group of Fundamentalists rented the local movie theater and opened a new church. The town was about 90 percent Catholic, and about 75 percent of the parishioners attended Mass every Sunday.

The Fundamentalists were financed by the national headquarters of their church. They also had the support of another Fundamentalist church in a town about 30 miles away.

"Visiting evangelists and students from a Bible college were coming to help them establish their new church and to knock on doors," Father Edward Petty recalls. "There were some fallen-away Catholics in their group, and they were more than aggressive in their entrance to our neighborhood. Every family of the Lutheran parish received a letter inviting them to leave the Lutheran congregation and join the 'Bible-believing' and 'fast-growing' church. But it was the Catholics of our parish they were really after. They made it plain that our town had been targeted because it was predominately Catholic, and their group had previously been successful in Catholic areas. We were 'ripe for the picking.' "

Fearing that his parishioners would fall prey to the on-slaught, the pastor and his assistant formed their own line of defense. They established Scripture-study and adult-education groups. But their main message was delivered from the pulpit at Mass. They incorporated stories of anti-Catholic prejudice in the United States and reinforced the fact that their town had been settled by the parishioners' ancestors in order to avoid anti-Catholic discrimination. They pointed out that after the election of John F. Kennedy as president, the reforms of Vatican II, and the growth of the ecumenical movement, anti-Catholicism had died down, but that the recent rise of Fundamentalism has brought a new wave of anti-Catholic sentiment.

Where Is THAT in the Bible?

The priests warned that Catholics are being taken in by Fundamentalists because they no longer know how to defend their faith when it is challenged. They used examples of Fundamentalist lines: *"We put our faith in Jesus, not in any church or sacraments." "Why go to a priest to have your sins forgiven, when Jesus can do it directly?" "The Bible says not to drink blood; that's why the Catholic idea of Jesus' body and blood in the Eucharist is wrong." "Show me in the Bible where it says to honor Mary so much?"*

The priests asked their parishioners if they could answer these questions. It was apparent that most could not. But the problem turned into a challenge. "We, in this parish, have a wonderful opportunity this year to take a good look at what we as Catholics believe and why we believe those things," the priests suggested.

They promised to address these issues throughout Lent.

"Folks were interested," Father Petty reported. "There was a sense of some competition in the air, sort of an our-team-versus-their-team attitude, which we downplayed, but it did interest some of the marginal Catholics."

Throughout Lent, emphasis was placed on Catholic beliefs and practices. Masses were packed. People asked for written copies of sermons, which they handed to the Fundamentalist missionaries who knocked at their doors. Record crowds attended the Forty Hours devotion.

"In spite of their money, personnel, and aggressive proselytizing, we did not lose a single parishioner to the Fundamentalists," the pastor reports. "We are not a perfect parish and never will be. But with God's grace, we are trying to be better Catholics and followers of Jesus Christ in our daily lives. Had we not had the courage and the ability to meet the Fundamentalist challenge in 1993, I shudder to think what the situation would be in this parish, with families split, people arguing, and who knows how many Catholics being lost to the faith."

Divided Families

Anyone who has experienced the conversion of family members or friends to a Fundamentalist church knows what Father Petty means when he talks about divisions and arguing.

"My brother joined a non-denominational church that preaches against Catholicism," one woman admits. "He tells me that the Catholic Church is the 'Whore of Babylon' and that the pope is the 'Beast.' He also claims that the Catholics added books to the Bible. I have heard this junk for years from others, so it was not new to me. But I was appalled to hear it from him. He worries about me because he is afraid I am going to hell for belonging to the Catholic Church. When I asked him if he thought our mother was in heaven, he would not answer. I asked him if he thought she had wasted her whole life in the Catholic Church and that the 10 years she taught religion were a waste. He would not answer. I sent him literature on these issues, but he is not comprehending any of it. My husband has advised me not to argue anymore. At first I thought I was helping, but now I have come to realize that my brother will never listen to me, so I have given up."

Aggressive efforts to convert others are interwoven into the Evangelical and Fundamentalist experience.

Are Catholics Christian?

Aggressive efforts to convert others are interwoven into the Evangelical and Fundamentalist experience. David Currie, a former Fundamentalist who converted to Catholicism, explains that from childhood he was taught that Catholics are not really Christians because they are not devoted to Jesus. He was told that Catholics believe they can earn salvation with good works. He was also taught that Catholics put their faith in the Church, the pope, Mary, and the saints — not in Jesus. From an early age, he learned subtle techniques on how to convert Catholics.

"Our Catholic acquaintances would have been shocked at how we talked of their beliefs in their absence," he admits. "It was not that we hated Catholic people, because we didn't. We believed, however, that the structure and teachings of the Roman Catholic Church were a false religion, only marginally connected with original Christianity. We saw Fundamentalism as the true Christianity. Catholics were spiritually lost, and we had to help them find Christ without being polluted ourselves. They needed to be saved. So we had contests in Sunday school to see who could invite the most 'unsaved' kids to church."

"I am 14 years old and my best friend is constantly questioning my faith," one teenager admits. "The sad thing is, I cannot find answers to her questions. The more she speaks to

How One Man Led Catholics Out of the Church

Before his conversion to Catholicism, Steve Wood worked as a youth leader, campus and prison evangelist, and pastor in a Protestant church. He admits to leading many Catholics away from the faith. He used a three-step formula:

- **Get Catholics to have a conversion experience in a Protestant setting.** "About five out of 10 people adopt the beliefs of the denomination where they have their conversion," he explains. "Most Protestant services proclaim a simple Gospel: Repent from sin and follow Christ in faith. They stress the importance of a personal relationship with Jesus and the reward of eternal life. Most Catholics who attend these services are not accustomed to hearing such direct challenges to abandon sin and follow Christ. As a result, many Catholics experience a genuine conversion. . . . Catholic leaders need to multiply the opportunities for their people to have such conversions in Catholic settings."

- **Give the conversion a Protestant interpretation.** He used what he calls a "touch and go" Scripture technique, in which he would quote various passages out of context to emphasize the Protestant interpretation. "In my experience as a Protestant, all of the Catholics who had a conversion in a Protestant setting lacked a firm grasp of their Catholic faith," he admits. "My selective use of Scripture made the Protestant perspective seem so absolutely sure. Over time, this one-sided approach to Scripture caused Catholics to reject their Catholic faith."

- **Accuse the Catholic Church of denying salvation by grace.** His primary motivation in converting Catholics is that he mistakenly thought that Catholics denied salvation was by grace. "Every Catholic I met during my 20 years of ministry confirmed my misconception that Catholicism taught salvation is by works instead of grace," he explains. This allowed him to use various Scripture passages to convince Catholics that their belief in salvation by works instead of grace would lead them straight to hell. (Steve Wood is the founder of St. Joseph's Covenant Keepers and is the author of *Christian Fatherhood*.

me, the more I feel that my religion is full of contradictions and loopholes. And the more I feel disconnected from it."

Cause for Concern?

These kinds of aggressive evangelization techniques extend to all age groups. "My sister, who is in college, was invited by her roommate to a Fundamentalist Scripture-study group," explains one young man. "Now she is posing some challenges to the Catholic faith. She disagrees with some of the dogmas. She opposes the pope's infallibility by saying the popes have done some very corrupt things in the past. She also opposes the idea of Mary's perpetual virginity, and she supports some of the reasons why the Reformation took place. She says we're not true Christians if we don't read the Bible and decide for ourselves. She says Communion is just a symbol. This has caused some strain between my brother and my sisters. My mother knows how my sister feels, but she is not terribly worried."

There should be some cause for concern when Catholics of any age are drawn into Scripture study, youth activities, or support groups that promote anti-Catholic teachings.

While "worry" might not be the best choice of words, there should be some cause for concern when Catholics of any age are drawn into Scripture study, youth activities, or support groups that promote anti-Catholic teachings.

"I left the Catholic Church because I could not reconcile myself with the Marian doctrines and the doctrine of purgatory," one young woman admits. "I attended a Baptist college, and although I had an awesome CCD experience, I was simply not prepared to defend those doctrines."

Steve Wood, a convert to Catholicism who founded the Family Life Center International and St. Joseph's Covenant Keepers, believes that Catholics should not participate in Fundamentalist activities unless:

- They have a firm grasp of their Catholic faith.
- They know their faith well enough to articulate it using Scripture and the Church Fathers.
- They have the maturity to realize that the most profound presence of Christ isn't necessarily found in the midst of loud noise and high emotion, but in the sacraments and in quiet moments of prayer and reflection.

A Grave Temptation

In 1989, the Catholic bishops of Alabama and Mississippi issued a strong statement warning that Fundamentalism constitutes "a grave temptation" to Catholics because it teaches:

- An unreasonable certainty about the meaning of Scripture texts regardless of their context.
- An overly simplistic certainty of salvation, achieved instantaneously upon acceptance of Christ as Savior.
- A deep sense of personal security, in often identifying the "American Way" with God's call and will.
- Intimacy with God in a relationship so personal that it effectively excludes others.

"As a community we have come to understand that the Bible is not a mere answer book for every problem," the bishops noted. "It is rather a record of God's loving and saving presence among His people. It is His call to us to become a loving saving presence of one another in the community that is the Church. We are called by the Church and God's Word to a fullness of life that develops the community and its members as people of God. That is why we cherish the sacraments so much and celebrate them with unparalleled joy. That is why the Eucharist, the greatest sign of our unity in sharing God's life, is the sun and center of our lives."

The Enduring Hunger for Jesus

In many cases, it is a hunger for the Eucharist that draws people back to the Catholic Church. "My husband and I left the Catholic Church after we were married and joined a non-denominational church," one woman admits. "It had so much to offer — friendly people, family programs, Bible study, social events. It was much different than the Catholic Church where you could be gone for months and no one would notice. But then one day I realized that this church made us feel good, but it didn't have the sacraments. I missed the Eucharist."

Substance of Belief

In other cases, Catholics begin to see that there is not as much substance in these churches as they first thought. Because they believe in individual interpretation of the Bible, they bring into ministry people without much formal education. It's not uncommon to find people with no training who run Bible studies and special ministries.

"I don't think they know the Bible all that well," one man admits. "My brother spouts the same passages all the time. The first few times you hear it, it sounds like he really knows what he's talking about. But after a while, it's just the same thing over and over."

It is important to understand that Fundamentalists did not come into prominence until the beginning of the 20th century. The movement arose as a direct result of the 19th-century rationalists, who began to question anything that could not be proven in a concrete way. At the same time, German Scripture scholars began to offer new interpretations of traditional Scripture texts. In the world of science, Charles Darwin's "Theory of Evolution" called into question the biblical accounts of creation. Since the Protestant Reformation was based in part on the premise that all authority is grounded in Scripture alone, any challenge of Scripture was seen by some Protestants as a threat. The Fundamentalist movement responded by taking the position that every word of the Bible is literally true.

This literal interpretation can be very appealing to people who are searching for answers. If someone is floundering around in a doubtful situation, Fundamentalism has instant attraction because it offers certitude. It puts the mind at ease by insisting, "This is what Jesus said. There can be no doubt about it. These are the words of Jesus."

Cafeteria Literalism

But there are specific instances where Fundamentalists do not take the words of Scripture literally. When you look closely at what Fundamentalists teach, you begin to see that individual interpretation of Scripture taken out of historical context can often distort the truth of what Jesus really said and did. They disregard or interpret certain

In the case of the Eucharist, for example, Catholics believe that the bread and wine become the Body and Blood of Jesus Christ. Fundamentalists believe that Communion is only a symbolic gesture.

passages as symbolic. In the case of the Eucharist, for example, Catholics believe that the bread and wine become the Body and Blood of Jesus Christ. Fundamentalists believe that Communion is only a symbolic gesture.

Catholics are sometimes attracted to these non-denominational communities because they are friendly and welcoming.

"I started going to a born-again church with some friends," one young man confessed. "At first, everything was really appealing. There was a very charismatic pastor and people were friendly, but before long, anti-Catholic statements began to creep into sermons and conversations. I began to study what Catholics really believed, and I was amazed at what I discovered. I was especially drawn to the Catholic teaching on the Eucharist. I had gone to Catholic school, but I never really understood what Catholics believe. Gradually, I began to see that the born-again church was mostly gloss and very little substance. Now my love for the Catholic Church is deeper and stronger than ever."

Does the Catholic Church Really Teach THAT?

The problem is that many Catholics do not take the time or the effort to investigate what the Catholic Church really teaches. "I think many young people question their faith when they begin to meet Evangelical Protestants," a woman points out. "Most of us received only minimal religious education. I was constantly told by my Fundamentalist friends that Catholicism wasn't true to the Bible. The truth is that I know very little about the Bible, so I always feel very self-conscious when I'm trying to defend the Catholic Church."

Parents often find themselves in the same situation. "My son is coming under the influence of Fundamentalist friends," one mother admits. "I found myself unable to answer many of his questions with support from some source other than my heart. I am working to understand the basis of Catholic beliefs, but I'm not sure that it would be a good idea to argue with him. I really don't know what to do."

In recent years, there has been an explosion of Catholic books, magazines, videos, and websites that explain what Catholics really believe and how to defend the Catholic faith. In many parts of the country, you can tune into Catholic radio or television broadcasts. Testimonies of Evangelicals and Fundamentalists who have converted to Catholicism also contain fascinating accounts of how they came to see the truth of Catholic teaching. Catholic Scripture study and faith-sharing groups are available in most dioceses. Find out what kinds of adult-education programs are available in your parish. If you feel that you don't know enough about your Catholic faith, then maybe it's time to learn:

- "I was angry at the Church and my parents for not educating me in my faith," one young adult admits. "CCD was a joke. But eventually I realized that I had to take some responsibility. I wasn't exactly an attentive student, and I didn't do anything to learn on my own. Sometimes it's easy to blame the Church or your parents, but the fault really lies with yourself."

- "I encourage reading apologetics, both modern and early," another young adult suggests. "It is important to be able to lay waste to anti-Catholic rhetoric."

No Guarantees

Keep in mind, however, that while learning more about Catholicism will certainly strengthen your faith, it will not guarantee that you can convince a friend or family member to return to the Catholic Church. "I have all the answers to the things the Fundamentalists preach," says Msgr. William Gallagher, "but in most cases I'm not dealing with people who are open to exploration of the truth. They have been trained to believe standard answers and criticism. They won't move from it. You can say anything you want, but it doesn't do a bit of good because they don't enter into the discussion with openness and goodwill."

Msgr. William Stanton agrees. For years, he has been actively involved in ecumenical dialogue, but he admits that he has always encountered difficulties with Fundamentalists. "The ecumenical movement is based on the respect different Christian denominations have for each other," he explains. "Even though I don't agree, I will respect what they believe. But the Fundamentalists will not respect what I believe. In any ecumenical group I have ever belonged to, the Fundamentalists refused to be a part of it. They refused to join, or in cases where they did join, they joined on their own terms — and eventually they left because they were not accomplishing what they intended. They have a missionary agenda and they will not back down."

Fundamentalist arguments tend to be very black-and-white. It is very difficult to keep these discussions on an intellectual level without some anger or resentment entering the conversation.

"It's hard to stand like a rock while someone blows around you like a storm," one mother admits. "It's hard to sit and take it. It feels like a slap in the face sometimes. The wound never seems to heal. Instead, it feels as if someone just keeps ripping the scab open."

Setting Boundaries

When this kind of Fundamentalist missionary zeal starts to happen in your home, your workplace, your circle of friends, or your neighborhood, most priests advise setting some boundaries. Msgr. Stanton tells people to say, "I respect what you believe, even if I don't agree with it. I also expect you to respect who I am and to treat me as I treat you. I am not haranguing you. I don't want you to harangue me."

"I've had this problem," admits Dan Collins of California. "First, you must respect the other person's views, then explain that you value your faith as much as they do theirs. You reach an agreement that you won't condemn them for their views and you don't expect them to condemn you for yours."

Father John Catoir tells the story of how his sister handled a Fundamentalist challenge by saying, "Of course, I'm saved. Jesus is the Lord of my life. Where do you get this nonsense? It's coming out of a complete lie. Catholics do accept Jesus Christ as our Lord and Savior. We do believe Jesus is the source of our salvation. You have your facts wrong. The information you have received about Catholics is basically erroneous and I will not discuss this further."

The key is to always present your position and set your boundary with an equal mix of firmness and love.

"I tried to challenge my friends on several points, but they didn't want to hear it," one woman confessed. "Now I just pray for them and try to lead by example. I show them how Christian a Catholic can be. They have finally stopped trying to convert me. I think that's progress. If they still think I'm on my way to hell, that's their problem."

"No one in the world can alter truth. All we can do is seek it and live it."

— St. Maximilian Kolbe

While aggressive proselytizing by Fundamentalists can cause problems, an even greater danger, especially for teens and young adults, involves the manipulative recruiting techniques used by cult recruiters. In the next chapter, we'll take a closer look at cults.

Chapter Notes

The pastor of a large Catholic parish in a small Midwestern town . . .: Edward C. Petty, "How My Parish Fought Off an Invasion," *This Rock* (February 1995).

"Our Catholic acquaintances would have been shocked . . .": David B. Currie, *Born Fundamentalist, Born Again Catholic* (Ignatius Press: 1996).

Catholics should not participate in Fundamentalist activities unless . . .: Steve Wood, *Family Life International*, Family Life Resources Online (March/April 1998; Vol. 4, Issue 2) at *www.familylife center.net/resourcesindex.html*.

Sidebar: *How One Man Led Catholics Out of the Church*: Steve Wood, "How I Led Catholics Out of the Church," *St. Joseph's Covenant Keepers Newsletter* (March/April 1998; Vol. 4, Issue 2).

Chapter 13

Cults

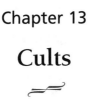

"We have not seen our daughter since she entered a cult five years ago. The cult has the legal right to keep her, and we have no rights to get her back. When and how do we stop this?" — S.B.

The Truth About Cults

Mention the word "cult," and memories of shocking headlines involving mass suicides probably come to mind. Most people agree that it is horrific, but they don't think it could ever happen to someone in their family. The real danger of cults, however, is much more subtle, and the people who think they are the most immune are sometimes the most susceptible.

Research shows that most cult members start off as "normal" people from all age groups, education levels, socioeconomic groups, and walks of life. It is estimated that there are more than 3,000 cults operating in the United States alone – some large and some small – and each has its own unique belief system. An estimated 5 million to 10 million people have been involved in these groups at one time or another.

When Cults End in Disaster

- In March 2000, over 900 cult members from The Movement for the Restoration of the Ten Commandments were burned, strangled, or stabbed to death inside a locked church in Uganda. The three most prominent cult leaders disappeared with the group's cash and possessions.

- In March 1997, 39 members of Heaven's Gate took their own lives with a mix of sedatives and vodka at the cult's headquarters near San Diego. They believed their souls would be transported to a UFO.

- In 1997, five members of the Order of the Solar Temple burned to death in St. Casimir, Quebec. They believed they would be transported to a new life on a planet called Sirius. Since then, murder-suicides by Solar Temple followers have claimed 74 lives in Europe and Canada.

- In October 1994, 48 bodies of cult members who burned to death were found in Switzerland. Five more bodies were found the same year near Montreal.

- In April 1993, Branch Davidian leader David Koresh and 80 followers — including 18 children — died by fire or gunfire, six hours after the FBI started filling their cult compound near Waco, Texas, with tear gas. The government called the deaths a mass suicide in fires set by cult members after a 51-day armed standoff.

- In December 1990, 12 people died after drinking poison in Tijuana, Mexico, during a religious ceremony.

- In November 1978, in Jonestown, Guyana, more than 900 followers of the Rev. Jim Jones died after drinking cyanide-laced punch. Jones, who was found dead with a bullet wound in the head, started the Peoples Temple in San Francisco before moving it to Guyana.

How Cults Recruit

Experts describe cults as groups or movements that have intense devotion to a person or to an ideal. There are "Christian" cults with modern-day prophets, "Eastern" cults with gurus, New Age cults with visionaries, political cults with charismatic leaders, survival cults with militaristic dictatorships, and doomsday cults that focus on the coming of the Apocalypse.

No matter what ideology a cult embraces, the leaders use manipulative methods of persuasion and control to recruit and retain members. It's not unusual for cults to dictate how members should think, speak, behave, react, and feel. Members are often isolated from family and friends. As former relationships are severed, members give their allegiance to the cult leaders, who often claim special status in the group.

The easiest targets for cult recruiters are good-natured people who tend to be trusting, open, looking for meaning in life, and experiencing some kind of minor stress such as the pressure of exams, a romantic breakup, a new job, a desire to make new friends, or family problems. Young adults are highly susceptible, and college campuses are prime places for recruiting cult members.

One Woman's Story

When Michelle Campbell was drawn into a religious cult during her junior year in college, her parents did not know what to do. "My parents were very upset," she recalls. "My father would tell me to make sure that this was not a Jim Jones cult. But this group was not dangerous in that sense. I didn't fear for my life. It was, however, emotionally, psychologically, and spiritually dangerous."

Michelle was raised Catholic but had stopped going to Mass as a teenager. "I never got it," she explains. "I never understood the deep truths of why we did what we did. I only remember learning about the rules."

When she was 16, her 21-year-old brother died. "It was a crisis for me," she says. "I began to wonder if there was a God."

At the age of 20, after much soul-searching, Michelle accepted Jesus Christ as her Lord and Savior in a Protestant church. "I experienced a lot of good changes in my life," she recalls. "I was never satisfied with answers that organized religion offered as solutions for the problems that a person can face from time to time. To me, Christ's message of compassion and unconditional love, along with the truth he taught and the grace we attain because of his sacrifice on the cross, was what changed my mind and heart and was the basis for my decision to follow him."

A Friendly Invitation

During her third year of college, Michelle transferred to a different school. She was studying for an exam one afternoon when a friendly young woman sat down on the bench across from her and asked what she was studying. She invited Michelle to join a religious group on campus and to attend a Bible study. This casual conversation marked the beginning of an involvement lasting five years and four months in what Michelle describes as a Christian cult.

The Bible study turned out to be a one-to-one indoctrination session with another member of the group. "I tried my best to approach the studies with skepticism," Michelle recalls. "I remember asking a lot of questions concerning the church and revealing that I already heard some negative things about them."

Michelle was told that she had to base her thoughts and feelings about the church on what the Bible says, and to make it her standard because it is black-and-white. She was not to go by other people's opinions. She was encouraged to review the notes from each Bible study. "What I realize now is that I was led and paced toward the right response for predetermined conclusions about the Scriptures the movement uses," Michelle admits. "I was led to believe I was making these 'awesome' strides in learning more about the Scriptures and God's will for my life."

Becoming a Cult Leader

Michelle eventually joined the group and became a "True Christian" and a "sister in Christ." Within three months, she became a "Bible Talk leader" and began to recruit new members for the group. "I served in different capacities of leadership within the next three years, from Bible Talk leader to assistant house church leader, and was responsible for leading a household," she recalls.

As a church leader, Michelle was instructed on what to say to the women in her Bible Talk. "We were always receiving direction on how to motivate our people," she explains. "We were told to meet with them daily, find out how their quiet times were, pray daily with them, and give them specific direction on how they could meet new people. Also, we were to find out what sins they were struggling with and find Scriptures in the Bible to 'convict' them. Many times I was directed to 'become a person's best friend' and to get to know as much as possible about them. In the leader's meetings, we would be asked to share information we had on a person so that the 'Evangelist,' or zone leader, could make sure to preach on it in the sermon in a given week. The person being recruited never knew that they were the topic of discussion in the meetings. Very rarely was God or Jesus mentioned as the one who ultimately moves a person's heart. On the outside, a non-member is paced and led to believe that God himself is speaking to their heart when they hear messages preached on the very thing they are struggling with or have done in the past. After a while, I began to realize that there was always an ulterior motive behind why I would get to know a person. It wasn't because I wanted to, but because I had to, in order to convert them into the group. Everyone outside the group was a potential convert, and we were told we needed to make every effort to convert them."

There were times when Michelle was taken out of leadership for not being obedient and submissive, or not performing to the cult's standards. She would be labeled as being spiritually weak, or judged and told that she was struggling with some sin. "I felt a lot of shame and felt like I had failed in not living up to expectation," she admits. "For a person to be taken out of leadership was looked on as being something adverse and negative to the group. I began to view God as a disciplinarian figure who was just waiting for me to mess up so he could criticize or punish me."

The Consequences

After six months, Michelle was academically disqualified from school because she was overloaded with responsibilities to the church. By the end of her first year, she was physically, mentally, and emotionally exhausted. On average, she got less than five hours of sleep each night. She became susceptible to catching cold or the flu. She moved seven different times within four years. Most of the time, she lived with four or five cult members, which allowed only rare moments of privacy. She went through five different jobs. Her finances were in ruins.

"I felt my joy and sense of self-esteem were eroding away the longer I stayed in the group," she admits. "Granted, there were some good things I felt I had learned over the course of time, but I had come to realize that I learned a very scripted way of how to speak to people inside and outside of the organization. I was taught to behave in a way that began to violate my conscience. I realized that I was doing things for the group, not out of a pure devotion to God but out of a unhealthy fear of punishment if I didn't. If I went a day without reading the Bible or praying, I began to feel something was wrong with me and that God was not pleased. As these feelings and questions began to rise to the surface more, I began to step back and observe the behavior and attitude of the environment I was in."

Michelle eventually broke away from the movement, but it was not easy. She is now the executive director of Reveal, a California-based organization to help cult members and their families through information, support, and intervention.

Advice for Families and Friends

The first thing Michelle tells the families and friends of someone who has been drawn into a cult is: "Don't panic. Stay calm. Educate yourselves. Keep the lines of communication open. Your son or daughter needs a link to the outside world. Family members and friends can be that link, but you will have to bite your tongue and love them unconditionally."

It's very important to understand that one of the techniques cults use is psychological isolation from families and friends. In a Christian cult, for instance, members are often told that they are making a radical response to the Gospel and that Satan will use people closest to them — family members and friends — to draw them away from the group. They sometimes use the following Scripture passages as proof:

- "Brother will deliver up brother to death, and the father his child, and children will rise against parents and have them put to death; and you will be hated by all for my name's sake" (Mt 10:21-22).
- "Henceforth in one house there will be five divided, three against two and two against three; they will be divided, father against son and son against father, mother against daughter and daughter against her mother, mother-in-law against her daughter-in-law

and daughter-in-law against her mother-in-law" (Lk 12:52-53).

If parents or friends criticize the group, the son or daughter immediately interprets those comments as persecution. If you accuse the group of being a cult, you walk right into a trap because the members are taught how to disassociate from criticism. You will get a blank gaze, and your son or daughter will literally tune you out. Many cults develop their own figures of speech and rote phrases that insulate members from the views of skeptics.

"When your son or daughter comes home to visit, allow them to go back to being their old selves without any pressure," Michelle Campbell advises. "Give them lots of good food. Let them sleep. Don't ask questions. Don't confront, blame, or criticize. Let them talk when they are ready. When I would visit my parents, I spent most of my time eating and sleeping because in the group I was not sleeping enough, not eating well, and working hard all the time."

Like Michelle, many young men and women begin to recognize the conflict between what they know is right and what they are manipulated into doing by cult leaders. They may begin to see hypocrisy or distortion of truth. Many eventually break away from the cult on their own — especially if they have maintained ties to family members and friends who love them.

Deprogramming

During the 1970s, there were sensational stories about the deprogramming process whereby cult members were kidnapped and forced to undergo therapy sessions in which the cult beliefs were psychologically deconstructed. These forceful tactics have fallen out of favor.

Today, some families attempt a peaceful intervention with voluntary exit counseling, which is a much calmer and more systematic approach that helps a person develop his or her own critical thinking skills. As cult members begin to recognize the manipulative tactics that were used to recruit and retain them, the psychological hold begins to unravel, and new connections can be made with family members and friends. Belief systems, values, goals, and independent thinking are gradually re-established.

"Don't ever attempt any kind of intervention unless you've done extensive research on the group and know how to counter their arguments," warns Michelle Campbell. "In most cases, families can't do it themselves. Parents may not be in the best position to help, especially if there are strained or dysfunctional relationships in the family. With young adults, it may be a pride thing. If they think they messed up, they may not want to go back to their parents for help. In most cases, an objective third party is the answer."

Some people emerge from cults with little or no psychological damage. Others may suffer from depression, a sense of alienation, low self-esteem, difficulty in decision making, lack of confidence, anxiety in social situations, shame or humiliation at having been drawn into a cult, grief over lost years, fear of making a commitment, excessive fear or paranoia, occasional panic attacks, as well as confusion over beliefs, values, and goals. If someone you love has been involved in a cult, make sure that he or she receives the necessary emotional and psychological treatment.

Warning Signs: How to Identify a Cult

- The group seems too good to be real.

- Members always agree.

- Everyone follows orders cheerfully with no complaints.

- The leaders have answers to all problems and concerns.

- Recruiting new members is an ongoing priority.

- Members are encouraged to donate or raise money.

- Members begin to feel guilty, ashamed, and unworthy.

- The members speak negatively about your former religion, family, friends, or lifestyle.

- The group expects you to make their meetings and activities your top priority before all other commitments, including school, jobs, or family responsibilities.

- The members warn that parents and friends cannot understand or help with religious, philosophical, social, or political issues.

- Scripture passages are twisted to reinforce the beliefs and practices of the group.

- The group considers doubts and questions as signs of weakness. You are punished if you persist in doubts.

- The leaders have different rights and abilities than other members.

- You are invited to join the group, but the members can't give you an overview of the purpose or goals of the group.

Combating Cults

The best way to combat cults is through education. Make sure that your teenagers and young adults understand how cults operate. Encourage your local high school to include cult-awareness programs for graduating high school seniors.

"There are a significantly greater number of colleges and universities today that are aware of cult activity on their campuses," said Ronald Loomis, education director for the American Family Foundation, the nation's leading cult-watch group. "And they are initiating programs to educate their students and faculty and staff about them."

Students at Georgetown University, for instance, receive a pamphlet titled "High Pressure Religious Groups," which describes those groups that use "persistent, manipulative, and often dishonest persuasion" to recruit members. Special training in spotting manipulative tactics is given to resident assistants, who serve as informal counselors to younger students in dormitories.

Stay Alert

Remind your family members and friends that no one wakes up one morning and decides to join a cult. They are seduced by normal, friendly people who invite them to join a wonderful, exciting group. Cults appeal to universal needs: the desire to belong, the need for orderliness, the assuredness of certitude, the dream of doing something worthwhile, the promise of unconditional love and acceptance. As the person enters more deeply into the cult, the reality of the outside world dissolves. Thoughts become twisted and re-formed into a new reality of programmed behavior. It happens gradually until the person is trapped.

Janine Marnien was lured into a cult during her freshman year at the University of Southern California. An enthusiastic young woman invited her to a non-denominational church service. Before long, Janine was attending, almost on a daily basis, Bible studies, services, and social activities,

---

A Checklist for Family Members and Friends: How to Protect Yourself from Cult Recruiters on Campus

- Before joining a club or a Bible study, ask people you trust who are not members of the group — friends, professors, counselors, or campus chaplains — for information about the organization.

- Research the group in the library or on the Internet.

- Ask questions. Be skeptical. Don't accept Scripture passages taken out of context as answers.

- Don't accept every invitation. Learn to say no!

- Complain to college authorities about harassment or violations of your privacy.

- Resist any efforts to isolate you from family and friends.

- Don't join any group that does not have realistic goals and expectations.

- Don't join any group that does not respect your beliefs, values, or goals.

and was forcefully recruiting other students. In addition to giving of her time, she donated a tenth of her income–about 30 percent of each meager work-study paycheck. "I just didn't realize what I had gotten into," she told *U.S. News & World Report*. What snapped her out of this mind control? One of the cult leaders told her she could not go home for her father's birthday.

Unconditional love and keeping the lines of communication open can make a difference.

While most families won't ever suffer the trauma of a loved one entering a cult, there is another force that is equally powerful and much more prevalent in today's society. In the next chapter, we'll take a closer look at the spiritual devastation caused by addictions.

Chapter Notes

"My parents were very upset . . .": From the author's interview with Michelle Campbell.

"I just didn't realize what I had gotten into . . .": Carolyn Kleiner, "Colleges Get Uneasy About Proselytizing," *U.S. News & World Report* (March 13, 2000).

Chapter 14

Addictions

"My daughter has stopped going to church. I think she drinks too much. She has a hard time keeping a job. I try to help her with money for food and rent. My husband and I fight over this all the time. But how could I abandon her?" — J.M.

No Room for God

One young man admits that he has no recollection of his mother ever taking him to church when he was growing up. His father, his godmother, and his grandmothers would make sure that he was at Mass every Sunday — but never his mother. "She never went to church," he recalls. "She was Catholic, but she never went to Mass."

The problem was alcoholism.

It's not uncommon for people who are struggling with addictions to have a low level of spiritual or religious involvement. Some are indifferent. Some are negative. Some are downright hostile toward God, the Church, and anyone or anything that has spiritual connotations. A close, intimate relationship with God — or even with another person — becomes impossible for addicted people to maintain because their overwhelming dependency on an addictive substance or an addictive behavior takes over their lives. The addictive agent becomes a false god. The addicted person acts in opposition to the most basic spiritual values. An addiction destroys a person's capacity for truth, sacrifice, self-discipline, and love.

Psychiatrist Gerald G. May, M.D., calls addiction "the sacred disease of our time." The effects of addiction can be physical, emotional, or mental, but the roots of the disease are spiritual.

It's not uncommon for people who are struggling with addictions to have a low level of spiritual or religious involvement.

"The spiritual aspect of addiction is truly a loss of self that ultimately results in a loss of the experience of all significant relationships," explains Eileen J. Stenzel, Ph.D. "As the disease of addiction progresses and preoccupation with the drug of choice intensifies, the addict, out of the need to protect the option to use the chemical substance, avoids anything that threatens that option."

The Cycle of Addiction

No one chooses to become an addict. Addictions develop gradually, which is why they are called chronic and progressive illnesses.

The cycle starts when a person discovers that a particular behavior or substance temporarily deadens emotional pain or physical discomfort and makes him or her feel good. Before long, however, the person begins to rely on the substance. Over time, the capacity to deal with life's difficulties becomes increasingly unmanageable. The person moves from occasional use to regular substance abuse as a crutch to get through the day. As usage increases, brain cells are altered — sometimes permanently. When this happens, the person becomes addicted.

"Our son told us he started smoking marijuana because it made him feel better when he was down," one couple admitted. "Gradually, he started using marijuana more and more. Eventually, he began to experiment with cocaine. Once he got hooked, he couldn't stop."

Who Gets Hooked?

Why some people become addicted and others don't is still not completely understood. Over 50 percent of people in the United States, ages 18 to 58, admit to having used marijuana or some other illegal substance at least once. Many people have also smoked cigarettes and consumed alcoholic beverages. Most do not become addicted.

In the past, people suffering from addictions were believed to be morally unstable, lacking in willpower, or possessed by some evil spirit. Today, experts believe that the causes of addiction are complex and multifaceted. They point to genetic predisposition, environment, body chemistry, and a reduced ability to deal with physical, mental, and emotional trauma. Not all of these factors can be attributed to every case. There is reason to believe, for instance, that a child of an alcoholic has a higher risk of becoming an alcoholic, but it does not happen automatically. Many adult children of alcoholics never have a problem with alcohol. On the other hand, there are cases of active alcoholics who have no family history of addiction whatsoever.

How One Handles Negativity

Psychologists James Whitehead and Evelyn Eaton Whitehead believe negative emotions are often a critical factor in addictions. "Although many adolescents experiment with alcohol and illegal drugs, only a small percentage develop debilitating drug habits that continue into adulthood," they explain. "Social scientists wanted to know why. They found the primary difference was how young persons handled their negative emotions. Adolescents who used drugs primarily to get rid of bad feelings were more likely to accelerate their use over time. Many of these teens became seriously addicted adults. In contrast, young people who developed effective ways to deal with or move beyond bad feelings tended to give up drugs altogether or limit their use to social occasions."

Types of Addictions

When most people think of addictions, the use of drugs and alcohol comes to mind immediately. The type of addictive agent may vary, however, depending on the individual. Prescription drugs, over-the-counter drugs, food, sex, nicotine, gambling, shopping, and even the Internet can be physically or psychologically addictive.

Dr. May adds to the list of addictions "relationships, power, moods, fantasies, and an endless variety of other things."

Some of these addictive agents are chemical substances; others are behaviors. Many people, for instance, are addicted to work. Their entire world revolves around their career. It becomes an obsession that is not easily broken.

"The workaholic experiences his anesthesia in the absorbing satisfaction he receives through working long hours and accomplishing more and more," explains psychiatrist Paul Meier, M.D. "The workaholic who tries to slow down without getting therapy feels tremendous pain and shame. He stays busy, to the point of exhaustion, and then wakes up the next morning and rushes back to work to avoid the pain of insight. Work acts as anesthesia from the pain."

The addictive agent also deadens people's ability to see what the addiction is doing to themselves and to the people around them.

"My daughter is addicted to painkillers," one man admits. "She lies. She steals. She makes life miserable for everyone in this family. I keep asking God to come into her life, but she has no interest in religion or in trying to help herself. She doesn't even think she has a problem."

The Problem of Denial

"The disease of addiction — any addiction — inevitably occurs hand-in-hand with the vexing phenomenon of denial," explains Father Harry C. Cronin, C.S.C. "If I am suffering

---

A Saint Who Struggled With the Effects of Family Addictions

St. Marguerite d'Youville (1701-1771), founder of the religious community commonly known as the Grey Nuns, was married to a man who suffered from a variety of addictive behaviors. "Drinking, gambling, and dancing filled his wretched days. . . . For his wife he now had no concern whatsoever. He was indifferent to her sufferings as if she were a person totally unknown to him."

from an addiction, I will not only deny that I am addicted; I will even deny that I am suffering."

Denial is an integral part of the disease and a major obstacle to recovery. It allows the person to continue under the illusion that nothing is wrong:

- Denial allows the person to find excuses to continue the addiction in spite of disastrous consequences.
- Denial keeps a person from seeing the physical, emotional, mental, or spiritual changes that have already taken their toll.
- Denial keeps a person from seeing how the addiction has affected family members and friends.
- Denial allows the person to hold on to the illusion that the behavior or the substance is the solution − not the cause − of whatever problems arise.
- Denial encourages comparisons to the stereotyped image of an addict and allows the person to conclude that his or her own situation isn't that bad.
- Denial leads a person to believe quitting is possible at any time.
- Denial convinces a person that he or she has everything under control.
- Denial is maintained by lies, rationalizations, justifications, and placing blame on someone or something else.

What's even worse is that people close to an addicted person also use denial as a coping mechanism. They ignore, minimize, or explain away all of the signs and symptoms. It's not uncommon for family members and friends to make excuses for the person's behavior.

"My husband would go down in the basement every night after dinner and drink himself into a stupor," one woman recalls. "Our children saw it before I did. When my son told me what was happening, I could not believe it. Now I can realize that maybe I didn't want to see it. I was unconsciously trying to maintain some sense of stability while everything around me was falling apart."

A Family Illness

Living with an addicted person affects the entire family. "When I was a young kid, I did not understand it," one man recalls. "I knew that my house was not like everybody else's house. I couldn't bring people home. I'd get up in the morning and my mother was never there. Breakfast for school? Never. I washed my own clothes. I took care of the house. I remember finding wine bottles and emptying them. My mother hid them everywhere. I wanted to help her. I wanted to do something to make it stop. I remember sitting in the window one time and crying because there was nobody home."

Secrets, lies, and loneliness destroy the bonds of love when there is an addict in the family. Anger and resentment fester. Fear, frustration, and feelings of betrayal become the norm. Faith in God and in other people erodes. There is no sense of inner peace. No hope. No trust. It's not uncommon for family members to become so obsessed with the behavior of the addict that they completely lose their sense of self. The lives of family members and friends become controlled by someone else's addiction.

"I was doing everything I could to help my son, but his drinking and gambling got worse, and he started to become

"There's an old saying: When fate throws a dagger at you, there are two ways to catch it — by the blade or the handle. Catch the dagger by the blade, and it may cut you, perhaps kill you. But if you catch it by the handle, you can use it to fight your way through whatever you are dealing with. When life throws a dagger at you, realize first that God is with you. Then grab it by the handle and ask God to help you use the awful experience to broaden and deepen your life." — Father Richard Zajac

abusive," one woman admits. "I talked to a priest who told me that I had to stop. My son was old enough to take care of himself, and he had to face the consequences for his actions. If I kept bailing him out, he would never change."

This kind of destructive "helping" is called "co-dependency," because without realizing what they are doing, family members enable the addict to continue in his or her downward spiral. They protect the addict from suffering the consequences of his or her behavior. They try to keep things smooth on the surface. But it's a no-win situation.

"As the disease pushes more, we give in more until we are tolerating things we said we would never tolerate and doing things we said we would never do," explains author and lecturer Melody Beattie. "Not only do many of us begin tolerating abnormal, unhealthy, and inappropriate behaviors, we take it one step further: we convince ourselves these behaviors are normal and what we deserve. We may become so familiar with verbal abuse and disrespectful treatment that we don't even recognize when these things are happening. But deep inside, an important part of us knows. Our *selves* know and will tell us if we listen."

One Woman's Diary

The diaries of Catherine de Hueck Doherty (1896-1985), who is currently being investigated for sainthood, create a fascinating portrait of a woman in a destructive, enabling relationship. Catherine's husband was obsessed with sexual relationships. At the time the diary was written, he had two mistresses, in addition to a number of casual relationships. Catherine blamed herself for her husband's infidelities. Her thinking became so distorted that she convinced herself that she had to accept everything her husband said or did, no matter how cruel, how unjust, or how immoral. She took jobs to support the family. She endured the gossip of neighbors and friends. She became so battered by her husband's verbal abuse that she began to compromise her own values. One day he asked her to lie to one mistress so that he could go to another. In her emotionally disrupted state, she did what he asked.

"Why do I have to go through all this humiliation of being a looker-on, a sort of helper-on," she wrote in her journal.

She wept uncontrollably. Thoughts of suicide plagued her. "Lord, you see how Boris, little by little, is killing my life," she wrote in her journal.

With the help of a wise Jesuit, she eventually came to see that she had to get away from the situation. She eventually went on to form Madonna House, an international lay apostolate that is centered in Combermere, Ontario.

Is Someone You Love Addicted?

- Do you worry excessively about the behavior of someone you love?

- Do you struggle with money problems because of what someone you love is doing?

- Do you ever lie to cover up for this person?

- Do you blame the person's behavior on his or her friends or co-workers?

- Are your plans frequently disrupted because of this person?

- Do you ever threaten to leave home if the person does not stop?

- Are you afraid that something you say or do will trigger an incident?

- Have people in your family been hurt or embarrassed by the person's behavior?

- Have holidays or special occasions been ruined because of this person's behavior?

- Have you ever thought about calling the police because of something this person did?

- Have you refused invitations because you are afraid of how the person will behave?

- Do you sometimes wonder if all of this is your fault?

- Has the person ever accused you of causing his or her problems?

- Do you find yourself feeling angry, confused, and depressed?

- Are you afraid to talk about this problem with a priest or counselor?
- Do you think that no one else would ever understand your situation?
- Do you sometimes feel that if this person really loved you, he or she would stop the destructive behavior?
- Do you sometimes feel as if God has abandoned you?

Breaking the Cycle

The first step in breaking the cycle is to understand that you did not cause the other person's addiction, you can't cure it, and you can't control it. You must accept the fact that you are powerless over your loved one's addiction. The only person you can control is you yourself. You must find the courage to step back and allow the addict to suffer the negative consequences of his or her behavior:

- It means not making excuses for the person.
- It means not lying or covering up.
- It means not giving the person money.
- It means not helping the person out of social, emotional, or legal problems caused by the addiction.

It's not easy to take a strong stand against someone you love. But until an addicted person begins to suffer the harmful effects of his or her addiction, there will be no motivation to stop.

Most people will not be able to face this kind of problem on their own.

Father Joseph Gatto, who has struggled with addictions in his own family, admits that this is not an easy process. "First, there has to be complete honesty," he says. "Second, you can't be afraid of anger because it's going to come whenever you begin to make changes in the status quo. The addiction will fight back. It might be rough for a while. You have to make sure you're taking care of yourself. You might have to walk out of the situation now in order to walk back later and make it better."

You Are Not Alone

Most people will not be able to face this kind of problem on their own. "Left by ourselves, we simply do not have the strength either to be honest with ourselves or to claim our dignity," explains Dr. May. "We must have help. Whether we like it or not, a large part of that help must come through other people."

Priests and pastoral associates may not have the training necessary to help you individually, but they will know where to refer you. If you want anonymity, call your local Catholic Charities office. Or contact a self-help group that specializes in supporting families and friends of people with different types of addictions. Most of these groups use a modification of the Twelve Step program developed by Alcoholics Anonymous. In the very first step, family members and friends admit that they are powerless over another person's addiction. They turn their lives and the lives of their loved ones over to God. Then they begin to focus on their own spiritual growth and development.

The Twelve Steps of Al-Anon

Al-Anon is a self-help group for people whose lives are affected by the alcoholism of a spouse, parent, child, relative, or friend. They adapted the Twelve Steps of Alcoholics Anonymous as the foundation of their program:

1. We admitted we were powerless over alcohol — that our lives had become unmanageable.

2. Came to believe that a Power greater than ourselves could restore us to sanity.

3. Made a decision to turn our will and our lives over to the care of God *as we understood Him.*

4. Made a searching and fearless moral inventory of ourselves.

5. Admitted to God, to ourselves, and to another human being the exact nature of our wrongs.

6. Were entirely ready to have God remove all these defects of character.

7. Humbly asked Him to remove our shortcomings.

8. Made a list of all persons we had harmed and became willing to make amends to them all.

9. Made direct amends to such people wherever possible, except when to do so would injure them or others.

10. Continued to take personal inventory and when we were wrong promptly admitted it.

11. Sought through prayer and meditation to improve our conscious contact with God *as we understood Him,* praying only for knowledge of His will for us and the power to carry that out.

12. Having had a spiritual awakening as the result of these steps, we tried to carry this message to others, and to practice these principles in all our affairs.

You may never be able to stop someone you love from destroying his or her life. But you can stop that person from destroying your life.

"My husband is an alcoholic," one woman admits. "I have finally accepted the fact that addictions are illnesses, and enabling is the absolutely worst thing that you can do. I love my husband, but I can't make him stop drinking. I can't make him go to church. I can't make him change."

When you reach this kind of surrender, you give up control and allow God's grace to take over. It's really a spiritual process. It's not unusual for families to begin to see little miracles all around them.

Addiction isn't the only situation in which you have to "let go and let God." This strategy can also help in situations where family members and friends have chosen lifestyles that are not in line with the moral teachings of the Catholic Church.

Chapter Notes

". . . the sacred disease of our time.": Gerald G. May, M.D., *Addiction & Grace* (Harper & Row, 1988).

"The spiritual aspect of addition is truly a loss . . .": Eileen J. Stenzel, "Recovery from Addiction," *Human Development* (Winter 1988).

"Although many adolescents experiment . . .": James D. Whitehead and Evelyn Eaton Whitehead, *Shadows of the Heart: A Spirituality of the Negative Emotions* (Crossroad Publishing Company, 1994).

". . . relationships, power, moods, fantasies . . .": *Addiction & Grace.*

"The workaholic experiences his anesthesia . . .": Paul Meier, M.D., *Don't Let Jerks Get the Best of You* (Thomas Nelson Publishers, 1993).

"The disease of addiction . . .": Harry C. Cronin, C.S.C., "The Addictions of Clergy and Religious," *Human Development* (Winter 1995).

"As the disease pushes more . . .": Melody Beattie, *Codependent No More* (Harper & Row, 1987).

The diaries of Catherine de Hueck Doherty (1896-1985) . . . .: Lorene Hanley Duquin, *They Called Her the Baroness: The Life of Catherine de Hueck Doherty* (Alba House, 1995).

"Left by ourselves . . .": Addiction & Grace.

Sidebar: *A Saint Who Struggled With the Effects of Family Addictions:* Marie Cecilia Lefebre and Rose Alma Lemore, *A Journey of Love: The Life Story of Marguerite d'Youville* (D'Youville College, 1990).

Sidebar: *1. We admitted we were powerless over alcohol . . .:* Reprinted by permission of Al-Anon Family Group Headquarters, Inc. The Twelve Steps of Al-Anon, as adapted by Al-Anon with permission of Alcoholics Anonymous World Services, Inc. ("A.A.W.S"), are reprinted with permission of Al-Anon and A.A.W.S. A.A.W.S. permission to reprint the foregoing material does not mean that A.A.W.S. necessarily agrees with the views expressed therein. Alcoholics Anonymous is a program of recovery from alcoholism only – use of permissible adaptation of A.A.'s Twelve Steps in connection with programs and activities which are patterned after A.A., but which address other problems, or in any other non-A.A. context, does not imply otherwise. Although Alcoholics Anonymous is a spiritual program, A.A. is not a religious program, and use of A.A. material in the present connection does not imply A.A.'s affiliation with, or endorsement of, any sect, denomination, or specific religious belief.

Chapter 15

Moral Dilemmas

~~~

"It's very hard for family members or friends to stand by and watch someone you love do things that you think are wrong." — J.M.

What Should I Do?

"An old friend came to see me a couple of months ago," a priest recalls. "He was upset because his son had moved in with a girl, and his daughter was already living with her boyfriend." "What should I do?" he said. "They are beautiful, talented, successful young adults."

"You don't have to approve," the priest told him, "but if you reprove too harshly, it could break the relationship. That is the fragility of the situation. You don't want to hurt the relationship."

It's not easy when family members and friends choose to act in ways that are not in line with the moral teachings of the Catholic Church. Your values and your own sense of right and wrong are challenged.

"I've been ridiculed by my family for trying to live a moral life and make moral choices," confessed one young woman. "I've found that I have to temper what I say so I don't sound preachy. I still hope that they will come around one day."

Breaking the Rules

There are many ways in which families, friends, and individuals can come into moral conflict. Dishonesty, cheating, choice of language, prejudice, defiance, unethical practices, or aggressive behavior are some examples. But the areas that seem to create the most dissension among families and friends often center on the sexual teachings of the Catholic Church.

"The values taught by the Catholic Church are so different from what is mainstream now," one young woman explains. "When I was in college, everyone I knew was sexually active. Most of us have been taught by the culture that our gratification is the most important thing. I don't think many of us question the Church about moral issues, because most of us don't know enough to even ask those kinds of questions."

Sex Outside of Marriage

Society today bombards us with sexual images and sexual information that people who grew up in the 1940s, '50s, and '60s never experienced in their formative years. Talking about sexual morality with teens and young adults is not something that many middle-aged or older people feel comfortable doing. Talking to teenagers about your expectations, your values, and the teachings of the Catholic Church is important, however. It's important to ask questions and be aware of the peer pressure and other influences that impact your family members. It's essential to know where teens are going, to set limits on certain activities, and to enforce curfews. These things lay a moral foundation. But ultimately, teenagers and young adults are going to make their own choices.

"As long as you are responsible when the children are being raised, you have fulfilled your obligation," explains moral theologian Msgr. Angelo Caligiuri. "There's commonsense wisdom in the position, 'As long as you live in my house, you follow my rules.' But once a person reaches adulthood and is accountable for his or her own actions, you are still a parent that is concerned and loving, and you can express your concern, but they go their own way. It's part of the 'letting go' reality of it."

> "If you keep silent, keep silent by love; if you speak, speak by love; if you correct, correct by love; if you pardon, pardon by love. Let love be rooted in you, and from the root nothing but good can grow."
>
> — St. Augustine

It's not easy, however. When family members and friends face a situation where someone they love is operating outside the bounds of what the Church considers morally acceptable, there is always tension.

"My friends think it's okay to have premarital sex as long as they are in a committed relationship," admits a young man. "I have tried to explain to them what the Church teaches, but they don't want to hear it."

Cohabitation

"My sister has been living with this guy and they just had a baby," another woman confesses. "They have no intentions of getting married. Our relationship has become strained because she knows that I don't approve of her lifestyle."

Msgr. Caligiuri recalls a distraught couple who sought his advice after relatives, who were not married, came to visit. The hosts offered separate bedrooms, but the pair ended up sleeping together in the same room.

"Should we have allowed them to stay?" the couple asked. "We didn't know what to do."

Msgr. Caligiuri assured them that they had done the right thing in offering separate bedrooms, but the unmarried couple obviously made their own decision, so the hosts were not morally responsible for their action. "You should be very clear that you accept them but that you don't approve of what they are doing," Msgr. Caligiuri explains. "You should continue to love them, with the hope that they will come to some rational understanding of what they are doing. How we communicate that is important."

You may feel angry, upset, disappointed, embarrassed, or ashamed. The bottom line, however, is that you make it clear that you want them to respect your values when they are around you. In other words, if your 22-year-old son wants to move in with his girlfriend, that's his decision; but when they come to your house, you make it clear that you do not expect the two of them to sleep together. It's okay to say, "You're always welcome in this house, but you are not welcome to do whatever you want in this house." It's a matter of decency and respect that should be mutual.

> **"When a child so dearly loved continually makes poor choices and develops attitudes foreign to a parent's values, it can be a harsh and dreadful experience for a parent to let go of the child they hoped for and to accept the child that they have."**
>
> **— Sister Joyce Rupp, O.S.M.**

Homosexuality

One of the most difficult situations family members and friends face is when someone they love admits to a homosexual orientation. David Morrison, author of *Beyond Gay*, which details his own struggle with same-sex attraction, conservatively estimates that there are as many as 12 million parents, siblings, and spouses who are affected when a family member "comes out of the closet."

"First, your children are still your children, and still love you," he tells parents. "If anything right now, your son (or your daughter) worries that you may love him/her less because of what they have told you. When I told my mother and father of my homosexuality, my mother cried and my father went into denial. Neither one realized that my telling them represented not my wish to pull away from them but to draw closer. Children do not tell their parents about their same-sex attraction because they want to hurt their parents but because they want to stop lying to them about something they consider very central to who they are."

Family members and friends admit that their first reaction is often shock, disappointment, embarrassment, and disbelief. It's hard when parents come to the realization that this child will not produce grandchildren, and in some cases, that the family name might not be carried on. There are concerns over what to say to other people and how this will reflect on other family members. Sometimes families wish they could turn back the clock and forget that this had ever happened.

"I remember working with one family," recalls Father Joseph Burke, S.J. "The father was very angry and demanded that his son stop being a homosexual. Of course, that is not possible. It's not something that the father can control."

What parents can do is learn more about homosexuality and what the Church teaches. In the past, the Church considered homosexuality "an intrinsic moral disorder." Today, the Church recognizes that a homosexual orientation is usually not a matter of choice and insists that people with same-sex attraction "must be accepted with respect, compassion, and sensitivity." However, because the Catholic Church teaches that sexual expression should take place only within marriage and must be open to the possibility of new life, the official Church teaching is that all people — married or not — are "called to chastity."

Focus on Three Things

While learning about official Church teaching is important, it does not prepare you for dealing with family members or friends who are gay or lesbian. Over the years, David Morrison has received hundreds of letters asking for advice. In response, he tells people to focus on three things:

1. **It's not your fault.** Part of the problem is that most parents worry about whether their child's same-sex attraction was caused by something they did or didn't do while their child was growing up. "I was raised by straight parents," one young man explains. "I went to Mass, read the Bible, said my prayers, was good to people, respected my family, and am gay. I wasn't taught to be this way by anyone. No person led me astray. I have no more ability to change my sexuality than the straight people I know. I did not choose this orientation."

2. **Loving your child doesn't mean you have to love everything they do.** Setting boundaries is important. Keep in mind that not all people with same-sex attraction are sexually active. If your child is involved in a relationship, you don't have to approve, and you don't have to allow public displays of affection in your home. One couple resolved this problem when their son wanted to bring home his partner to meet the family. "We already had the experience of one of his older sisters wanting to bring her boyfriend into the house and sleep in the same room with him," the mother explained. "We nixed that, so it wasn't too hard to tell [our son] that we would meet the boy but that if they stayed overnight he was going to have to stay in his old room and we could put his friend in the nice back guest room."

3. **It's not the end of the world.** While it may seem as if your whole world has changed, the reality is that nothing has changed. This is still the same son or daughter that you knew and loved before you knew the truth. Their gifts, talents, intelligence, creativity, sense of humor, and personal goodness are still there. Your son or daughter still needs your love and your support. They also need your honesty. They need to know that even if you don't approve of their choices, you still love them. "Although some parents have found it difficult and worry that it might be counterproductive, most of the parents I

> **"I have been driven many times to my knees by the overwhelming conviction that I had nowhere else to go."**
>
> **— ABRAHAM LINCOLN**

have met who have reconciled themselves to a child's having a degree of same-sex attraction have done so by being honest, even when it hurt," David Morrison observes.

Advice of the American Bishops

In a pastoral message to the parents of homosexual children entitled "Always Our Children," the American bishops' Committee on Marriage and Family urged people to draw on their reservoirs of faith, hope, and love. They offer the following recommendations:

> **"If you truly want to help the soul of your neighbor, approach God first! With all your heart, ask him to fill you with love — the greatest of all virtues. With it, you can accomplish what you desire."**
>
> **— St. Vincent Ferrer**

- Accept and love yourselves as parents in order to accept and love your son or daughter.
- Do everything possible to continue demonstrating love for your child.
- Urge your son or daughter to stay joined to the Catholic faith community.
- Recommend that your son or daughter find a spiritual director/mentor.
- Seek help for yourself, perhaps in the form of counseling or spiritual direction, as you strive for understanding, acceptance, and inner peace.
- Reach out in love and service to other parents who may be struggling.

- As you take advantage of opportunities for education and support, remember that you can only change yourself; you can only be responsible for your own beliefs and actions, not those of your adult children.
- Put your faith completely in God, who is more powerful, more compassionate, and more forgiving than we are or ever could be.

Divorce

Another life crisis in which families and friends have no control is when couples divorce.

The word itself means a separation, a division, a pulling apart of people. A union that was supposed to last forever comes to an end. It is the death of a relationship, the death of dreams, the death of a commitment, and it is often accompanied by feelings of anger, rejection, betrayal, guilt, and immense loneliness. It is not uncommon for everyone involved to go through a period of mourning.

"The biggest thing for me was: How can we have a child who is getting a divorce?" one parent admits. "How could this happen in this Catholic family?"

One of the biggest myths that continues to be perpetuated in Catholic families is that once a divorce decree is final, the couple is automatically excommunicated. This is not true. Horror stories abound in which people stay away from the Catholic Church because they think that they are barred from receiving Holy Communion.

"My husband left me, and my relatives told me that as soon as I received my divorce papers I was automatically excommunicated," one woman recalls. "I stayed away from the Church for three years before I found out it wasn't true."

"The ignorance of others also kept me away from the Church," a middle-aged man admits. "I was told that my divorce prevented me from being a Catholic. The best thing I ever did was go and talk to a priest who told me there was no reason that I couldn't come home!"

As long as divorced people have not committed any serious sins, they are still in good standing with the Church and may continue to receive the sacraments.

Divorce and Remarriage

Problems arise when a person remarries outside the Church. Because divorce is not recognized by the Church, the first marriage is still considered valid. Since civil re-marriage is not recognized, couples who remarry without an ecclesiastical annulment "cannot be admitted to the Eucharist."

"After I remarried, I played the organ at Masses for six years without receiving Communion, and I can tell you that it hurts," one man admits. "There is nothing quite as dev-astating as exclusion from the Eucharist."

Whenever someone remarries outside the Church, family members and friends ask the same questions:

- Should I attend the wedding?
- Is my presence saying, "I agree with what you're doing"?
- By not attending, am I closing the door on reconciliation?

These are difficult questions that do not allow for simple answers.

"We look at it this way," one couple confesses. "We may not like it that our son isn't getting married in the Church, but it beats having them move in together. Second, to refuse to attend seems rude and not very Christian. Third, if we keep encouraging them to pursue their annulments, there's a chance that they might be able to reconcile this with the Church at a later date. In other words, we're going to the wedding."

Going to the wedding does not necessarily mean that you approve. Your son or daughter will know that your presence is a sign of your love — not necessarily of your endorsement of the choices that were made.

If family members decide they should not go to the wedding, they should never take a position of self-righteousness, anger, or rejection. There should be an honest statement that they can't go in conscience because it is against what they believe. Maybe they can compromise and only go to the reception. Or maybe they could have a quiet family dinner for the new couple at home.

Whatever a family decides, it's important that the people involved remain true to what they believe is right. The couple knows that they are moving outside the limit of the family's belief or value system, but they are going to do it anyway. The child may live to regret the decision, which is an important reason why it's essential for families to maintain contact.

> "If you see someone sinning, pray to the Lord and say, "God, forgive me for I have sinned."
>
> — SAYINGS OF THE DESERT FATHERS

"I have a dear friend who remarried about six years ago," one woman explains. "Her parents refused to attend the wedding. I even went by and talked with them, but they absolutely refused. It caused so many hard feelings that they are now cut off from their grand-children, who are being raised Catholic. My friend's hus-band is in the process of getting an annulment, and they hope to have their marriage validated by the time their oldest daughter makes her First Communion. I don't know whether or not they will reconcile with her parents. It caused a lot of hard feelings."

Whatever you decide, remember how important it is to keep the lines of communication open. "Don't risk los-ing a child or grandchildren over this," one priest advises. "Let them know that you don't approve. Your presence at the wedding is not going to make them think you've changed your mind. But it will show them that even though you disagree, you still love them."

If someone in your family is in this situation, you might want to suggest the possibility of looking into an annul-ment. Like the subject of divorce, the annulment process in the Catholic Church is plagued by myths and miscon-ceptions. In the next chapter, we'll unravel the truth about ecclesiastical annulments.

Chapter Notes

"When a child so dearly loved . . .": Joyce Rupp, O.S.M., *Praying Our Goodbyes* (Ave Maria Press, 1988).

"First, your children are still your children, and still love you.": David Morrison, *Beyond Gay* (Our Sunday Visitor, 1999).

In response, he tells people to focus on these three things: Ibid.

"We already had the experience of one of his older sisters . . .": Ibid.

In a pastoral message . . .: "Always Our Children: A Pastoral Message to Parents of Homosexual Children and Suggestions for Pastoral Ministers" (NCCB/USCC, June 1998).

". . . cannot be admitted to the Eucharist": Pope John Paul II, *Familiaris Consortio* (1981), no. 84e.

Chapter 16

The Annulment Process

―⁓

> "I think my brother turned against Catholics because
> he remarried outside the Church and this was his way
> to justify it." — V.F.

Indissolubility of Marriage

Msgr. William Gallagher is the pastor of a booming Catholic parish in Orchard Park, N.Y. A few miles down the road is a booming non-denominational church. Msgr. Gallagher estimates that 60 percent of the members of the non-denominational church are former Catholics.

"From what I can see, they have a lot of our people who are in second or third marriages that can't be resolved with the marriage tribunal," he observes. "That's part of the attractiveness of those places. Since they don't have a doctrinal anchor, they can pretty much develop the churches the way they want to. They can make up their own rules, and they do."

One of the great ironies in many of these churches is that they hold to a literal interpretation of Scripture except in certain instances. One of the passages that many of these churches sidestep contain some of the most basic teachings of Jesus that prohibit divorce and remarriage (Mt 5:31-32, Mk 10:11-12, Lk 16:18).

The Catholic Church defines marriage as a "covenant by which a man and a woman establish between themselves a partnership of the whole of life." The Catholic Church recognizes marriage as a sacrament and teaches that a valid sacramental marriage is indissoluble except by the death of one spouse.

"Unfortunately, not every couple who marries has what it takes to make a lifelong commitment," admits Father John Catoir, who is an author, a canon lawyer, and a tribunal judge in the Diocese of Paterson, N.J. "Today's divorce statistics indicate that many couples lack the necessary maturity and the moral resolve needed for a truly valid marriage."

Annulments

The Catholic Church has become more lenient in granting annulments over the past 20 years because of a deeper understanding of psychology, addictions, abuse, and so on. It recognizes that people who marry may not have been capable of making a permanent commitment due to immaturity, psychological problems, and other reasons.

"When my son was divorced, I told him right from the start that he could get an annulment," one mother confesses. "But he wasn't going to church at that point, so he didn't care. I told him that someday he might want to remarry in the Catholic Church. He wouldn't even hear of it. My former daughter-in-law was also upset that I had suggested an annulment. She thought it would mean that the two years they were together were for naught."

These kinds of misconceptions are common. "What became a conflict in my family was my mother seeking an annulment," one woman admits. "The annulment made everyone angry. I didn't understand the process, and she was, at the time, incapable of explaining it to us."

Myths About Annulments

There are a lot of myths about the Catholic annulment process. Here are some facts:

- Receiving an annulment does not mean that a loving marital relationship never existed.
- The children do not automatically become illegitimate.
- Annulments do not have to be processed in Rome.
- Annulments do not cost thousands of dollars.
- A person does not need "influence" to get an annulment.
- The annulment process does not take "forever."

An annulment is simply a declaration that when the marriage vows were exchanged, there were impediments that prevented one or both of the partners from making a mature, adult commitment to the marriage.

"If it is clear that this is not a true marriage, the Church not only has the right but the duty to annul it," explains Father Catoir. "What appears to be a valid marriage is not always so. Sometimes circumstances exist which are not obvious to the average person. Sometimes there is an element of fraud or psychological incapacity present."

What Makes a Marriage Valid?

For a marriage to be valid, canon law requires the following:

- Both parties must possess sufficient use of reason and a mature understanding of the matrimonial rights and duties.
- They must have the ability to assume the obligations of marriage without any psychological impediments.

- They must freely consent without any pressure or force.
- They must be willing to have children.
- There must be no fraud or deceit.

If these elements are not present before the marriage or at the time the vows are exchanged, grounds for an annulment may exist.

For example, a rushed marriage when the bride is pregnant raises the question as to whether both parties gave free consent without pressure or force. Marriages that last less than a year often indicate a serious lack of maturity. A history of addictions or psychological disorders may indicate an inability to assume the obligations of marriage. An emotional compulsion to marry, such as a desire to get away from one's family or family pressure to marry, could raise questions as to the validity of consent. Any circumstances where there was no commitment to stay in the marriage for life, including former romantic attachments or suppressed gay or lesbian tendencies, would be possible grounds for annulment. Maybe one or both partners lacked the ability to make sound decisions. Any case of physical or emotional abuse would raise questions as to whether there was sufficient understanding of the marriage covenant.

Other Requirements for Validity

The Catholic Church also insists that a marriage between two Catholics must comply with the requirements set in canon law. This means that the wedding must take place in a Catholic church, with a priest presiding or with a dispensation that allows Catholics to be married by a Protestant minister or a rabbi. Marriages of Catholics in a civil ceremony performed by a justice of the peace or in a non-Catholic ceremony without a dispensation are not recognized by the Catholic Church.

"My best friend was married by a justice of the peace," a young man explains. "The priest told him that he didn't have to go through the whole annulment process because the Catholic Church never recognized the marriage in the first place. It was just a matter of paperwork, and the tribunal gave him a certificate saying he was free to marry in the Church."

How Families and Friends Can Help

While family members and friends can be supportive of someone who is seeking an annulment, they cannot petition the marriage tribunal to open an investigation into the validity of another person's marriage. Only the former spouses can do that. Family members and friends can help by letting the couple know that the annulment process is a possibility. They can refer them to a priest or a member of the marriage tribunal. They can also offer to be witnesses in the annulment process.

"The purpose of the witnesses is to support and verify the petitioner's testimony," Father Catoir explains. "The credibility of the people involved is very important. Friends and family members can serve as character witnesses."

Serving as a Witness

"I was more than willing to cooperate," one mother admits. "I saw that it was not a sacramental union. I didn't have to appear at the tribunal. In fact, all the paperwork was done in another city. They sent me a questionnaire. I wanted to talk to the priest who sent it to me. I didn't have to, but I wanted to get details about it. He told me that he thought my daughter had grounds for an annulment. They may be called judges, but they are not judgmental and they don't condemn you. They want to help people. They are not the enemy."

Father Salvatore Manganello, the judicial vicar for the Diocese of Buffalo, admits that many people are apprehensive when they are asked to be witnesses in the annulment process.

"Basically, all we want is for you to be objective and truthful," he says. "If people don't feel like they can write answers to the questions or they aren't sure how they want to word it, we can always set up a time when we can talk on the telephone or in person."

The questions are generic: Please describe the background of the man and the woman. Describe the courtship. Were there any problems in the courtship? Were there any premarital difficulties? Were family members and friends in favor of this marriage? If not, why?

The tribunal does not tell the witnesses what the grounds for the annulment are or what kind of information the judge is seeking. The tribunal takes the testimonies and tries to determine whether a certain relationship met the qualifications of marriage as understood by the Catholic Church. The tribunal does not make a judgment about either person.

"I answered the questions honestly, and I never blamed either person," one parent says. "It was like writing a case history. I wrote 8 to 10 pages. I said there was immaturity on both parts. Throughout every question, I repeated that I thought these two young people were immature and that neither was prepared for marriage. They were attracted to each other, but they had no idea what it meant to be married. If two people are not mature, how can they commit themselves for the rest of their lives? Blame has nothing to do with it."

The annulment process is always confidential. The only people who can have access to the information are the tribunal staff and the two parties to the marriage. Neither party is ever given copies of the paperwork. If they want to see what is in the file, they must go to the tribunal office and read the file in the presence of a staff person.

"Witnesses sometimes ask if we can keep certain information confidential from the couple who are seeking the annulment," Father Manganello notes. "For instance, it sometimes happens that there are things a witness would not want us to tell the parties because it may affect their relationship. We could hold out that piece of information. We wouldn't be able to hold out all of their testimony. But that one piece could be dropped out if it would seriously affect the relationship."

Pain and Healing

There is no question about the fact that the annulment process can be painful. It dredges up hurt feelings, bad memories, negativity and feelings of anger or resentment. "We have to try to get beyond the anger, but it isn't always easy," Father Manganello explains. "Sometimes people are angry and hurt because they didn't want the divorce or the annulment. Some people are upset over unacceptable divorce settlements. Sometimes we see people who have been traumatized by the relationship. A lot of times the process gets all tied up with one side against the other. Their family members and friends may feel the same way. When the anger is justi-

"Sometimes, people are angry and hurt because they didn't want the divorce or the annulment."

— FATHER SALVATORE MANGANELLO

fied, we try to explain that what happened is not justifiable. It should not be allowed. The Catholic Church does not expect marriage to be that type of relationship, and we cannot condone it. But we can't change what has already happened. In the end, we have to do our best to help them deal with it."

"When my son's annulment was granted, it was such a healing thing for me," admits one woman. "It really allowed me to let it go. After all the mistakes I made in raising my children, here was a tribunal that had the grace of the Lord to grant or not to grant an annulment. They looked at this case and said these kids were too immature. The marriage was not a sacrament. That made me feel good. The kids' lack of maturity had nothing to do with me!"

Chapter Notes

The Catholic Church defines marriage as a "covenant by which a man and a woman establish . . .": Code of Canon Law, Canon 1055.

Chapter 17

Angry at the Church

⌒

"I guess I fit the picture here. I've been hurt and disappointed by the Catholic Church. I've tried other churches, but I still haven't found any place where I feel like I belong." — S.L.

The Priest and the Farmer

There was a story circulating in 1997 at World Youth Day in Paris about the family of a Canadian priest whose parents were farmers in central Ontario. One year a hailstorm destroyed their crops. The father went to the bank to get a loan to keep the family solvent until the next year, but the banker in town kept stalling on the paperwork. Eventually, the father asked the banker why he wouldn't approve the loan.

It turned out that the pastor of the parish in town was a major stockholder in the bank. The pastor was pressuring the banker to foreclose on the farmer's property. It made good economic sense. The family was a poor risk. If the bank foreclosed, the bank would actually make money when it resold the farm. The fact that their own pastor was pushing this agenda was hard for the family to accept.

The father went to a neighboring town and got a loan from another bank. But the family still faced the difficult question: "Can we continue to go to Mass at this parish, knowing what this priest tried to do to us?"

The mother said, "We will go to Mass here. The Church and the Eucharist are bigger than the pastor is. We will stay with the Catholic Church."

Many years later, after their son was ordained, he was stationed in a town where the former pastor was now in a nursing home. His mother asked if he had gone to see the pastor yet. The young priest said, "No, I don't want to go and see him."

The mother said, "You must. Forgiveness is bigger than he is."

Remember the Bigger Picture

When someone is hurt by someone or something in the Catholic Church, it is difficult sometimes to see that the Church is bigger than our own individual hurts. The last straw is often an experience of hurt, lack of support, lack of compassion, or rejection by a priest, parish person, or fellow Catholic. Horror stores abound:

- "I left the Church because of something that happened in the confessional," one woman admits. "The priest was rude, crude, sarcastic, and mean. He twisted my words to say things I did not mean. He even resorted to name-calling. When I started to cry, he looked at me with scorn and contempt. I felt as if I were a terrible person and that God hated me."

- "I spent 12 years in Catholic schools," a man explains. "With the exception of one nun that I had in third grade, two nuns in high school and one priest, I have nothing but contempt for those people. I had a learning disability that made reading very difficult. I was constantly called stupid. They allowed other kids to make fun of my stuttering. The hypocrisy was horrible. I know most of them are now dead, but I am left with a lot of bad memories."

- "My husband says the Church left him," another woman explains. "He never felt comfortable with the changes after Vatican II. He argued with our pastor after Mass one morning and hasn't been back since."

- "My mother left because of something that a priest said to her," a young man recalls. "She is still wounded, and she has cut herself off from the source of healing. As time goes on, she becomes more bitter."

Unintentional Hurts

Bishop Henry J. Mansell, bishop of Buffalo, tells the story of his unsuccessful efforts as a young priest to encourage one of the teenagers in the parish folk group to sing a solo at Mass. One Sunday, he decided to force the issue and announced, without warning, that this young woman would sing during the presentation of the gifts.

The teenager sang, and her voice was so magnificent that people in the pews had tears in their eyes. Elated, he went over to thank her during the sign of peace. "Drop dead!" she replied.

"She was only kidding," the bishop admits, "but there are times when priests hurt people without intending to do any harm."

Feeling Betrayed

In other instances, it's not so much a feeling of hurt that people experience as it is a feeling of betrayal:

- "My children stopped attending Mass while going to a Catholic high school," one man admits. "The principal (a priest) ran off with the vice principal (a nun) and had twins four months later. Before it happened, my children would relate stories about their goings-on. I would reprimand them, saying things like, 'You can't spread gossip. It can't be true. Don't ever let me hear you say these things again!' They complied with my command, until the day the priest and the nun took off together. Three of my daughters have returned to the Church, but they are very skeptical. The fourth is a professed atheist."

- "We just had a very popular priest from our parish leave the priesthood to get married," another woman explains. "It was awful. Rumors and gossip were flying around. No one knew what to believe."

Situations like these are never easy. Some people say the feelings of loss, abandonment, and frustration are similar to those experienced by families that are suffering through a divorce. "How could someone do this to us?" they ask.

Other people have questions. They want to know if the sacraments a priest administered are still valid. They want to know if the former priest is still bound by the seal of the confessional. The answer to both of these questions is yes.

What most people don't realize is that this was probably an excruciatingly painful decision for a priest or a religious in this situation. As vicar of priests in Cleveland,

Father Donald Cozzens had to meet with priests who were in the process of leaving. "We both understood that his leaving would be seen by many as incomprehensible, and by some as a betrayal of trust at best and an act of infidelity at worst," Father Cozzens recalls. "I found these meetings both poignant and muted. We spoke in tones heard in a funeral home. The atmosphere was charged with a certain sobriety – and a penetrating sadness."

On one level, you might be able to get someone to admit that people change, circumstances change, and that even the Catholic Church can change. But when a person feels deeply hurt or betrayed by someone or something in the Church, they sometimes reach a point where they no longer believe that it is possible to reconnect.

The Fish Experiment

Several years ago, researchers conducted experiments with a walleyed pike. They put the fish in a glass aquarium and fed it every day. After a while, they inserted a glass divider in the tank that separated the fish from the food. Every time the fish tried to get food, it would crash into the glass divider. Eventually, the fish gave up trying. At this point, the researchers removed the divider, but the fish never again attempted to get the food. It eventually died of starvation, even though the barrier was gone and the food was waiting.

This is the same thing that happens to many fallen-away Catholics. In order to break down this kind of negative conditioning, people must be willing to risk crossing the imaginary line that separates them from what could be a source of spiritual nourishment:

- "I was really angry at the Church for a time," one woman admits. "I thought it was an evil institution run by corrupt people who only sought to exploit others through their faith. All I ever heard was 'Thou shalt not . . .' I just couldn't accept what the nuns said because it was nuns saying it. I had to rebel and go searching for other truths. I explored every "ism" and "osophy" and "ology" there was. Then about a year ago, I decided to give the Catholic Church one more chance. Actually, God was giving me yet another chance, and I am finally home. The Holy Spirit opened my ears and let the light flood into my heart."

- "I sometimes wish that we could have a Reconciliation Sunday or Mass where people could bring their hurts and burn them in a symbolic gesture after the priest has apologized in the name of the Catholic Church for any past hurts," one woman suggests. "I think it would bring healing. I once read that forgiving isn't forgetting. It's remembering and letting go."

Forgiveness

Most experts agree that forgiveness is a good thing. Forgiveness allows people to drain the poison out of the wound. It puts a stop to the repetitious thoughts that destroy peace of mind. It restores a person to spiritual, mental, and emotional wholeness. Forgiveness sets people free.

"If we are prisoners of our past hurts — no matter how profound and how deep — we are prisoners nonetheless," says Msgr. Robert Zapfel. "The Lord came to set prisoners free. He meant people unjustly behind bars, but sometimes those bars are bars of resentment, hatred, lack of forgiveness, lack of compassion, and lack of charity in our lives. The freedom to be open to God's love means being free from those kinds of prison bars as well."

The Church Is Bigger Than the Local Parish

If family members or friends have been hurt by someone or something in the Catholic Church, encourage them to separate the person or the thing that hurt them from the Church and the sacraments. Encourage them not to cut themselves off from a source of spiritual nourishment because of something a human being said or did. One woman encouraged a friend to try another parish by drawing an analogy to grocery shopping: "The guy at the local supermarket completely humiliated me one day," she said, "but I haven't stopped shopping at the supermarket chain, only at that particular location."

> **"Forgiveness simply means getting down off the seat of judgment and releasing those who have offended you from your own hostility and anger."**
>
> **— JOHN MICHAEL TALBOT**

Abuse and Apologies

An isolated incident is one thing. It's a different story when there is a pattern of abuse or when a situation is so negative that large numbers of people are affected. "I have watched a warm, loving parish community deteriorate into hostility since our new pastor arrived," one man confesses. "His negativity has drawn everyone into a downward cycle. There is only one Catholic parish, and it would take an hour to get to another one. Some people are doing that. Others are going to one of the Protestant churches in town. My story is just one of many."

In cases like these, it is wise to let the bishop know what it happening. It's your parish too, and you have a right as well as a responsibility to express your concerns. The bishop also has a right to know what is happening in the diocese. When there is injustice or hurt or human frailty, the Church may need to apologize.

In March 2000, Pope John Paul II asked forgiveness for past and present sins committed by Catholics in the name of the Church. He apologized for sins against Christian unity, for the use of violence in attempting to defend the truth, for sins against Jews and people of other religions, for sins against women and against the weakest and most vulnerable members of society. This unprecedented act was repeated by many bishops around the world who asked forgiveness for the human failings in their own dioceses.

> "I am aware of the many ways the Church has failed me, and I have failed her. Yet I claim this Church as mine. She is my mother, my home. A broken home, yes! Broken because you and I are broken."
>
> — **SISTER MACRINA WIEDERKEHR, O.S.B.**

The very fact that the Church has survived for 2,000 years in spite of its obvious human weaknesses is an indication that the Holy Spirit has kept the Catholic Church alive and growing. God's forgiveness and mercy tell us that it is important to recognize hurts, to apologize, and then to encourage everyone to move forward.

Dealing with disappointment, pain, and anger is never easy. Sometimes, however, it is not the Catholic Church that fuels people's anger. Sometimes, people get angry at God.

Chapter Notes

"We both understood that his leaving . . .": Donald B. Cozzens, *The Changing Face of Priesthood* (The Liturgical Press, 2000).

Chapter 18

Angry at God

~~~

"After my mother died, everyone in our family stopped going to church. I think we were all mad at God. We felt like our prayers weren't answered." — P.Z.

Blaming God

Sister Margaret Krantz, F.M.D.C., is a certified bereavement counselor. She says it's not unusual for people to stop going to Mass after the death of a loved one. Sometimes the problem centers around not wanting to go back into the church where the funeral was held because the memories are too raw. More often than not, however, the real reason is a deep seated anger at God:

- "A friend of mine lost her infant daughter to sudden infant death syndrome," one woman says. "She is so mad at God that she no longer goes to church. She cannot forgive God for the grief that has befallen her."
- "When my dad died, I was confused and angry," another woman admits. "I had put all my faith in God, prayed to the saints, prayed the Rosary faithfully, but he still died. I was angry at God, the saints, everyone."

Sister Margaret admits that some people carry angry feelings toward God for years. But death isn't the only loss that people grieve.

"After my parents got divorced, my mother stopped going to church, which leaves me with no one but myself to go," a teenager confesses. "I think my mother is mad at God."

People also struggle with anger at God over other problems: a debilitating injury, a serious physical or mental illness, an act of violence against an innocent person, the loss of a job, a forced early retirement, a failed business venture, a deep disappointment caused by a friend or family member, an unexplainable accident, or some natural tragedy that destroys homes or lives. At times, painful memories from the past unleash angry feelings.

Why? Why? Why?

Pat Gordon was a faithful Catholic until 1986, when she became angry at God over painful childhood memories that started to surface. "The more I learned, the more bitter and angry I became," she says. "For the next 13 years, I railed against God, asking him, 'Why? Why? Why?' As you may have guessed, I got no answers."

Pat stopped going to Mass. "Going to ANY church was out for me," she admits. "I always started crying and had to leave."

When bad things happen, most people want to know why. They assume that if they knew the reason, acceptance would be easier. But that is not always the case. One young mother knew the medical reason that her baby died in her womb, but it didn't help ease the pain of miscarriage. Sometimes the tougher question is: How could a loving God allow this to happen?

Father Richard Zajac, a hospital chaplain, remembers being called to anoint a patient about to undergo surgery for a bleeding aneurysm. The prognosis was not good. The family had gathered in the waiting room. "And what made this particular situation even more distressing was the fact that the day before, they had all attended a funeral," Father Zajac recalls. "The daughter of the man having surgery had taken her life. Here was this group of people in the waiting room, reeling from the grief of losing a daughter and a sister, and now in the throes of even more tragedy. Five hours later, their worst fears were realized. The surgery was unsuccessful. The patient died. It was for me another example of the uncertainty of the human experience. They didn't deserve to have one tragedy thrust upon them, to say nothing of a double disaster."

The Mystery of Suffering

There are no satisfactory answers to tragedies like these. When Sister Joyce Rupp, O.S.M., began teaching a course entitled "Praying Our Goodbyes," a young widow, who could not forgive God after her husband's death, advised Sister Joyce not to automatically assume that all people receive strength from faith. It's hard for some people to turn to God as a source of strength when they see God as the source of their suffering.

"That is why the mystery of suffering must be considered when one is reflecting on the losses in life," Sister Joyce admits.

Father John Catoir entered into this mystery when his mother died during his second year in the seminary. "I was praying so hard for her to live," he recalls. "I thought it would be my mother's great desire to see me ordained, and I couldn't understand why God did not answer my prayers. One of the major pillars of my faith was the faith and confidence I had that if I prayed hard and really believed, the Lord would be there for me. When this didn't happen, it opened up the possibility that there may be other situations when I would need God's help and he would not appear. It took about five or six months until I began to think of it from a different perspective. My mother was in pain. She was suffering. What advantage would there be for her to go through two more years of agony? She could see my ordination from another base. Maybe she would be applauded in heaven in a way that she wouldn't be on earth. It was a matter of trusting that God knows what is really best."

It's Okay to Feel Angry

When Father David LiPuma was in his first year of the minor seminary, his mother died. A few months later, his father died from a massive heart attack. "I stood in that hospital room and I screamed at God," he recalls. "I was out of control. I was so angry. It wasn't fair. I was giving my life to God, and God was taking away the people closest to me."

In looking back, Father LiPuma realizes that after the initial outburst, he did not allow himself enough time to work through his anger. Now he tells people that it's okay to be angry at God. "It's okay to say, 'I'm angry because you took this person away from me. I'm angry because this person is sick. I'm angry because you allowed this to happen. I'm angry because someone hurt me very badly. I'm angry because it feels as if my life is falling apart.' It's good to say those things out loud. God's shoulders are bigger than we can ever imagine."

Anger is simply an emotional response to something that seems like an injustice. Whether the injustice is real or imagined, a person still feels anger, and ultimately the anger has to be addressed. Part of the problem of being angry at God is that people feel deeply wounded, but at the same time they tell themselves that there is something intrinsically wrong with getting angry at God. Instead of dealing with the anger, they try to bury their feelings. Suppressed anger does not go away, however. It festers beneath the surface. Sometimes it manifests itself as depression, nervous tension, self-pity, or a victim mentality. Sometimes the smoldering anger explodes in angry outbursts over things that are completely unrelated. Sometimes people try to deaden the pain with pills, alcohol, drugs, sex, or some other compulsive behavior.

The Need to Talk

"That's why it's important for people to talk to family members and friends about their feelings," Father LiPuma insists. "It's only when people can open up and let the anger drain out that they begin to heal. They need to find someone that they can be totally honest with, someone they can talk to, someone who is not going to try to answer what they're feeling or try to fix their feelings. They don't need someone preaching to them. They need someone to listen with an open heart."

It's unfortunate, but not uncommon, for grieving people to find the kind of support they need outside the Catholic Church. "I started going back to the Catholic Church after

> **"The truest sympathy is found in those who, with the strength of love, come out of the sunshine into the gloom and dimness of others, to touch wounds tenderly, as though their own nerves throbbed with pain."**
>
> — Bishop Fulton J. Sheen

my husband died, but I still felt empty," one woman explains. "I ended up meeting a woman who invited me to her church. They read the Bible. I asked for forgiveness for being angry at God. I accepted Jesus Christ as my Savior. From that day on, I was a new creation. My life has changed. I have no more panic attacks. I am not angry. I am not bitter. I am not envious. I have forgiven those who have wronged me. My daughter has also received Christ. We are part of a faith community now, with God as our foundation. We pray together. We laugh together. We are learning from the Lord and have such a love for him that it's amazing."

Grieving people need support. Sister Joyce calls it *kinship*, and she insists that it is much more than just another word for friendship. It is that deep bonding that allows two people to feel a certain unity of heart, mind, and spirit. "We draw strength from just knowing that the other is there and that she or he understands, that we can draw energy from one another in our time of need and return it just as generously when the time is called forth," she explains.

Becoming a Kindred Spirit

Increasingly, Catholic parishes are starting bereavement support groups for people who are struggling with the loss of a loved one. If you have family members or friends who are angry at God for any reason, try to be a kindred spirit for them. Assure them that anger is a normal part of the grieving process. Help them find ways in which they can turn to God. It might mean going with them to a different parish. It might mean helping them find a priest or a bereavement counselor. It might mean praying with them when they feel as if they can't pray by themselves. It might mean encouraging them to express their pain.

"I advise people to keep telling God how they feel, because it's in that dialogue that they will come to some peace with it," Father LiPuma says. "That's called prayer, and it's some of the best prayer because you are speaking honestly from your heart. God can handle it."

> **"I have sometimes felt closest to God when I have been furious."**
>
> **— MADELEINE L'ENGLE**

Sometimes it helps if you can just sit with another person in silence. No one expects you to have all the answers. God does not need you to defend or protect him. God does need you to walk with family members and friends in faith. Sometimes it is the silent presence of a faith-filled person that makes a difference in the lives of others.

Father Peter Daly recalls going to a hospital to pray with the family of a man who had just died from a massive heart attack. "They were divided into two groups, literally and figuratively," he recalls. "One group was comprised of practicing Catholics, real believers; the others were nominal believers at best. Everybody was sad, of course. But the believers were calm. The non-believers were almost overcome by grief. Faith made the difference."

A Silent Witness

If you find yourself in a similar situation with family members or friends who are angry at God for whatever reason, maybe God is calling you to be a silent witness. Maybe you will be the instrument that will bring your family member or friend to a deeper level of faith. Maybe you will be the one who can accompany someone who is blinded with grief on a journey back to God's love.

> "Unless we learn the meaning of mercy by exercising it toward others, we will never have any real knowledge of what it means to love Christ."
>
> — THOMAS MERTON

"Kinship is not always easy," Sister Joyce admits. "As we walk with others who are working through a loss, we may get very tired or impatient with their seemingly slow progress. We may be irritated with their self-orientation or their constant heavyheartedness or their strong hold on anger or breaking into tears at the most unpredictable times. It may take real effort to keep standing by them, but how necessary it is to do so. We need to be faithful. This is the Gospel love which gives without expecting in return. We also need to extend invitations to growth, but when these invitations are not accepted we need not feel rebuffed or rejected. These refusals are simply indications that the grieving one is not yet ready to move on."

In God's Good Time

At times, healing and reconciliation come in ways we least expect. For Pat Gordon, who was angry at God over painful childhood memories, healing came at the bedside of her dying mother, who had not spoken or acknowledged any family members. "The day before she died, she smiled when I told her I was there," Pat recalls. "I was the last one to see her alive. I feel God gave me a great gift in that I saw my mother, she knew I was there, and we had a private good-bye."

After the funeral, Pat started to attend daily Mass. "I received the Sacrament of Reconciliation and am moving ahead," she says. "I now pray the Rosary every day and praise God in little prayers throughout the day. I am gaining something I have always wanted: inner peace."

Chapter Notes

"*And what made this particular situation even more distressing . . .*": Richard Zajac, *Life Injections* (CSS Publishing Company, 1998).

"*That is why the mystery of suffering must be considered . . .*": Joyce Rupp, O.S.M., *Praying Our Goodbyes* (Ave Maria Press, 1988).

"*We draw strength from just knowing . . .*": Ibid.

"*They were divided into two groups, literally and figuratively . . .*": Peter Daly, "Jesus Said, 'Fear Not,' " *Catholic Digest* (October 1999).

"*Kinship is not always easy . . .*": *Praying Our Goodbyes*.

THE REALITY

"Loving trust means an absolute, unconditional, unwavering confidence in God, even when everything seems to be a total failure."

Mother Teresa of Calcutta

When family members and friends leave the Church, there are only two possible outcomes: either they eventually come back to the practice of the Catholic faith or they don't.

The question that family members and friends often ask is "What can I do?"

In this section, we'll take a closer look at what you can do when a loved one is away from the Church. After all is said and done, however, you still have to face reality. In the last two chapters of the book, we'll explore the reality that:

❖ Sometimes Catholics Come Back to the Church
❖ Sometimes They Stay Away

Chapter 19

Sometimes Catholics Come Back to the Church

"The unfortunate thing is that there is no simple recipe to coming back. Each person has a unique story and situation." — Michelle L. Smith

Hunger for the Eucharist

A woman from Texas admits that she left the Catholic Church in 1970 because she felt as if nobody cared about her. "It seemed to me at that time, all the Church was interested in was deep pockets, baking cookies, and having kids, none of which I had or was interested in," she exclaims.

During the 20 years that she was away from the Church, she essentially cut off her connection to all religious practices. "I never stepped inside a Catholic or a Protestant church except for funerals," she says.

The turning point in her story came when she started watching the Eternal Word Television Network and began to feel a deep hunger for the Eucharist. She wanted to go back to the Catholic Church, but she did not want to return to the cold, unfriendly parish that she remembered.

"Fate stepped in," she says. "I wanted to sell my house, and by the grace of God, the realtor was Catholic. During the course of several discussions, he invited me to meet a priest who would listen to me. From that day on, the Church has opened up for me. The realtor became like a brother to me. The priest has become my best friend, and I have worked with him doing missions on 'Healing Life's Hurts.' "

"We are hard-hearted and close-minded for years. Then comes a moment of vulnerability and mercy. We break down and break through."

— **FATHER RICHARD ROHR, O.F.M.**

The most amazing part of this story is that she ended up returning to the same parish that she had left 20 years before. She is now a eucharistic minister and a lector.

"I have lots of friends at daily Mass," she says. "It has been quite a journey, but thankfully, one that turned out well for me."

Those Who Return

While God is at the center of each person's decision to return to the Church, the circumstances surrounding people's return are as varied as the reasons why they left. Twenty years ago, sociologist Dean R. Hoge grouped people who return into four broad categories:

1. **Marriage Life Returnees:** These people are strongly influenced by a spouse or concern for their marriage.

2. **Family Life Returnees:** Their motivation stems from concern for their children's religious upbringing and a desire for religious solidarity in the family.

3. **Guilt-feeling Returnees:** These people feel guilty about leaving the Church. They sometimes feel nostalgic about their religious upbringing, and they

long for the good things they remember about growing up Catholic.

4. **Seeker Returnees:** These people search for an answer to a spiritual need or a sense of purpose in their lives.

While most people do not mention spiritual motivation as the primary reason for coming back, in 41 percent of all cases they mention it in conjunction with some other influence. This was confirmed in a recent survey of young adults. "The most common reasons for returning were feelings of spiritual need (26 percent) and concern about family life and religious education for their children (24 percent)," the study concluded.

Birth of Children

Alice McDermott, a fiction writer, who was raised in an Irish Catholic family in New York, admits that her return to the Catholic Church coincided with the birth of her children and the questions that suddenly surfaced: "How will they be educated, how will they learn to be good people, how is it I took so long to realize my parents did a pretty decent job after all?"

"Twenty years ago, no one could have convinced me that I would send my children to Catholic schools," she confesses, "but of course, now, that's where they are. Because I want them to have the ballast of faith, because I want them to understand the importance of the life of the spirit, because I want their moral education to have a context that exceeds human logic and understanding and gives to the whole of life that shapeliness I had once thought could only be achieved, momentarily, by art. Because I know there will be times in their lives when they will need the Church."

The Meaning of Life

Father Joseph Burke, S.J., believes the central issue faced by people who are away from the Church is: What gives life meaning?

"A lot of people have lost that sense of meaning," he explains. "They begin to ask themselves, 'What is my life all about? Why do I get up in the morning? Why do I do what I do?' As a parent, a spouse, a sibling, or a friend, your role is not to restore that meaning, but to enable the others to find meaning for themselves. You can help the other person re-find spirituality and re-find faith. You can enable that person to reconnect. You can't force. You can't take on responsibility for someone else's actions. You can't demand that they come back. You can't pressure them to come back. But you can help them to reconnect."

Looking for Signs

Sometimes it's just a matter of watching for signs that someone is interested. It might take the form of a question or a comment. You might notice a slight interest in a book, a pamphlet, a television show, or something that happened in the news.

"It has been my observation that the families who find it easy to see the signs are those who have kept a warm and loving relationship while yet making known their disappointment — not anger — that is felt when a loved one leaves the Church," observes a pastoral associate who works with fallen-away Catholics. "It seems to me that we must acknowledge that God does not stop loving a person who makes this decision and that we ought not look upon the time away as sinful. For whatever reasons, the individual has tried to find faith somewhere else and will come back to the Church with greater love and longing than ever before when the Spirit beckons. In my opinion, it's the 'prodigal son' story all over again. The son who stayed behind because of loyalty never came to know the great love and understanding the father is capable of displaying. The younger son's journey, though seeming to take him away from the father, was in reality teaching him what valuable things he had lost, and his return was vastly more meaningful."

What to do when you begin to see these early signs is another matter. Father Gary Bagley suggests that you proceed with caution. "The biggest sign is when someone starts asking questions," he says. "If people are wrestling and fighting, it means the hook is in their mouths. When the hook is in, let it sit there for a while and go slow. Let the process take its course. It's the old story about watching the butterfly break out of the cocoon. If you help the butterfly, it dies because its wings aren't strong enough. Its wings get strong by the struggle it has with the cocoon. Sometimes the hardest thing to do is sit back and watch the struggle. It's like watching little kids learn how to walk. You let them take their own stumbling steps. You just keep them away from open stairways and sharp objects. It's the same here. Let the person wrestle with it themselves."

"I was born and raised Catholic, and then I left the Church," explains Mark Sturgis. "I became a born-again Christian and joined the Assemblies of God and other Fundamentalist churches for 24 years. I just came back to the Catholic Church, and I know the Holy Spirit led me on this journey to teach me some very important lessons about following God's will and what it truly means to be conformed to the image of Christ. Trust in Christ, and he will see your loved ones through this."

The Miracle of God's Grace

What you will witness in the process is the miracle of God's grace. It's not uncommon to see people's lives change radically in the process of returning to the Church.

"I was gone for 10 years, but you wouldn't know it by my faith today," one man admits. "Absence did make my faith stronger because I found what it meant to return. I did not know it at the time, but my destiny and my purpose in life were unfolding. I know now that my absence made me recognize right and wrong."

> "Grace is needed to turn a human being into a saint, and anyone who doubts it does not know what a saint or a human being is."
>
> — BLAISE PASCAL

Many Catholics who return to the Church speak about missing the Eucharist and its significance as truly the Body and Blood of Christ.

"Receiving Jesus in the flesh is a thrill *nothing* can match," one woman explains. "Most people know in their hearts that there is truth in the Catholic Church, and that's why they keep circling around. That's why the thirst may fade, but it never goes away completely."

Some people miss the devotions to Our Lady or the saints. "St. Francis of Assisi and Our Blessed Mother led me back," another man admits.

Some miss the Catholic rituals, the prayers, and the sacramentals.

"Older people tell me they missed the smell of incense," says a nursing-home chaplain. "People's senses play a big part in what is remembered in fondness, and these all combine to draw individuals back. I believe it is the Spirit reminding them of a time when reverence and awe were very much a part of their lives. As they use their intelligence to question and doubt, it is their minds and not their hearts which pull them away. On the other hand, it is the love and awe and beauty of the Catholic Church that pulls them back."

Sometimes fallen-away Catholics will take the initiative and attend a Mass on their own. If they are welcomed warmly by the priest or the parish community, it almost always cements the relationship.

"One Sunday, I had nothing to do, so I thought, 'Has the Church changed any in the past decade?'" recalls a middle-aged man. "I opened the Yellow Pages and found a parish on a street with a familiar name. I attended and was heading out the door when the priest shook my hand and mentioned that he had not seen me before. He asked what I thought about the Mass. I told him the music sounded great. To make a long story short, I have been singing there for 20 years."

"Kindness has converted more people than zeal, science, or eloquence."

— MOTHER TERESA OF CALCUTTA

"We need to make sure that our parishes are waiting with open arms, much like the father who sees the prodigal son and runs to meet him," one woman suggests. "We need to make sure that's the kind of reception people will receive as they come back home."

Apprehension of Some

Most people admit that while they feel drawn back to the
Church, they also feel a strong pull in the opposite direction that seems to paralyze them. "I haven't returned to the
Church yet," says a woman from Colorado, "but I am con-
sidering it. I'll tell you one thing, however. If I find the
same old garbage I've seen in the past, I'll just do my praying on my own. I like the rituals of the Catholic Church. I
do not like the behavior of the clergy or the congregation.
At any rate, if I choose not to practice my religion, I won't
convert to another. I feel like this was the religion I was
born into, and good or bad, it's as much a part of who I am
as the color of my eyes or what kind of ice cream I like."

Michelle Smith understands this apprehension. "I have
a friend who was raised a Catholic but fell away from the
Church many years ago," she says. "She is on the fence about
returning. Her strongest reluctance is mainly out of fear, confusion, and embarrassment (among many other things). I
have shared with her that no matter what, God never stops
loving us. God is always merciful. I have also shared that
God longs for us to open our hearts to him. If we have been
away, he will openly welcome us back. I have suggested that
she speak with a priest and have so far hit with resistance. I
suggested as well that she pray and place her concerns in
God's hands. However, she has such a high brick wall in front
of her that she's having a hard time getting over it."

Msgr. Tony Attea believes that part of the fear people
face is not knowing what to do at Mass — especially if they
have been away from the Church for a long time. Some people
are afraid that they will be rejected or treated like an outcast.

If you sense that someone wants to return to the Church but feels apprehensive, you can help the person overcome fear by extending an invitation to join you at Mass.

"If you invite people to go to Mass on their own, they won't go," Msgr. Attea says. "You have to invite them to join you at Mass on Sunday. They need someone to be with them. If you invite people to come, after a few times, they may begin to think about becoming a member. If they are afraid to come to Mass, invite them to parish functions so they can meet people. Spaghetti dinners, softball, or other parish activities that are non-threatening will let them begin to think about formal membership. Always invite them to family religious events like baptisms, First Communions, or confirmations. No badgering, just invitations."

The 'Right' Parish

Sometimes the best thing you can do is help someone "shop" for a parish. As kids, many Catholics were taught that the Church is unchanging and always the same everywhere. But that's not true. The Catholic Church is universal, it is diverse, and it is constantly changing. In every diocese, you will find parishes with different personalities. It's up to each individual to find a place where one is nurtured and a place where one's talents can be used. You can help people find a parish community where they feel at home.

"There is always a way to return when the will do to so is strong enough," one woman insists. "I have met old people who are away from the Church for various reasons. Each time I spoke to a priest about their situation, the priest would be helpful in finding a way to bring them back to the Church."

The 'Right' Priest

When referring someone to a priest, keep in mind that there are different types of fallen-away Catholics and that they look for different traits in a priest. Some people look for a priest who is warm and nurturing. Others want a priest who will engage in philosophical or intellectual discussions. Some simply want someone who can answer their questions. Others want a priest who will pray with them. You can't expect one priest to be able to meet every person's needs.

"Some folks want to be led back to the Church," explains Father Bagley. "They are genuinely hurting people who need to be guided back. I'm better with the folks on the opposite end, who left the Church because they didn't want to be over-directed. These folks want to wrestle with questions and struggle with their anger."

Making the Connection

Most experts agree that the return to Catholicism is strongly associated with the person's relationship with a sympathetic spouse, friend, priest, or teacher. "Beginning when I was 25, things started to happen and I slowly made my way back toward God without even knowing it," John Knutsen explains. "In August of that year, I made friends with a wonderful priest, and he helped me limp back toward the Church. I am still working at it. To make a long story short, this has been a remarkable year, and over the past few months I've had a number of priests and brothers tell me that I have a vocation. So there's hope. If I can come back, anyone can!"

When offering advice on any aspect of the Church, it's important to make sure your facts are correct. Paul Couturier of Worcester, Mass., suggests that you pick up some good books or pamphlets on the Catholic faith. The *Catechism of the Catholic Church* is an excellent resource. "I personally recommend the *Catholic Answer* series," he says. "Ask your loved one to read them and pray! If they refuse to read these materials, as Jehovah's Witnesses will do, then pray some more!"

The Power of Prayer

Prayer is always the best — and, sometimes, the only — resource that people have when a loved one leaves the Church. "I have great faith that my son will return to the Roman Catholic nest," one mother says. "But I can't put a 50-year-old head on his 28-year-old shoulders. It's a waiting game and a praying game too."

Sometimes people see the results of their perseverance and prayer. They witness amazing transformations when their loved ones return to the Church:

> **"God does not demand that I be successful. God demands that I be faithful. When facing God, results are not important. Faithfulness is what is important."**
>
> **— MOTHER TERESA OF CALCUTTA**

- "I lived without God in my life and it wasn't pretty," admits a former fallen-away Catholic. "I didn't have any inner peace. Now that I have him, I have found that my anger, negativity, and just plain hatefulness are gone. I pray and ask him for his guidance and strength. I don't care what anyone says, my life and my attitude toward everything is so much better than it was. It wasn't easy, but it is possible to come back."

- "I just came back to the Church," another woman says. "I'm so glad that I waited until I was an adult to be confirmed. I attended RCIA and learned more about my religion than I did in six years of Catholic school. I now belong to a Scripture-study group and I love it."

It would be wonderful if every story in this book could have a happy ending. Life isn't like that, however. Sometimes people leave the Catholic Church and never come back.

Chapter Notes

Twenty years ago, sociologist Dean R. Hoge grouped people who return . . .: Dean R. Hoge, *Converts, Dropouts, Returnees: A Study of Religious Change Among Catholics* (United States Catholic Conference, The Pilgrim Press, 1981).

While most people do not mention spiritual motivation . . .": Ibid.

"The most common reasons for returning . . .": Mary Johnson, Dean R. Hoge, William Dinges, and Juan L. Gonzales, Jr., "Young Adult Catholics: Conservative? Alienated? Suspicious?" *America* (Vol. 180, No. 10; March 27, 1999).

"How will they be educated . . . ?": Alice McDermott, "Catholic After All," *Catholic Digest* (July 2000).

Chapter 20

Sometimes They Stay Away

"Just because something is impossible doesn't mean you shouldn't do it." — Dorothy Day

Inviting People to Come Home

For years, Petronilla Amantia agonized over relatives who had fallen away from the practice of the Catholic faith. "They never went to Mass on Sunday," she recalls. "They would come to Mass for special family events, but they wouldn't go to Communion. My kids kept asking why some people in the family were religious and some people weren't."

One day, Petronilla saw an article in the newspaper about a program that the Franciscans in New York City had started as a way of inviting fallen-away Catholics to "Come Home." She realized that she probably would never be successful in bringing home her own family members, but she might be able to help other people return to the Church.

> **"If you're going to care about the fall of the sparrow, you can't pick and choose who's going to be the sparrow. It's everybody."**
>
> — **MADELEINE L'ENGLE**

Her interest led to the start of a Come Home program in the Diocese of Buffalo that has helped thousands of alienated Catholics return to the practice of the faith.

Throughout the United States and Canada, particularly in large metropolitan areas, increasing numbers of dioceses and parishes are offering special programs or information sessions specifically designed to invite lapsed Catholics back to the Church. The structure of these programs may vary. But whether the program is called "Come Home," "ReMembering," "Landings," "Another Look," or "Alienated Catholics Anonymous," the goal is always the same: to provide a warm, non-judgmental environment where people can explore without pressure the reasons they left the Church and whether or not they want to return.

> **"The Holy Spirit sends every baptized person to proclaim and bear witness to Christ. It is a *duty* then and a *privilege*, since it is an invitation to cooperate with God for the salvation of each individual and all humanity."**
>
> **— POPE JOHN PAUL II**

If you have a family member or friend who is away from the Church, you might want to get involved in this type of ministry. If nothing exists in your parish, consider starting some kind of outreach.

If you're reading this and thinking that there's no way you could start a parish outreach to fallen-away Catholics, there are still ways that you can help bring people back to the Church. It's called *evangelization*, and it stems from Jesus' final message in the Gospel of Matthew, where he commissioned his followers to "Go therefore and make disciples of all nations" (Mt 28:19).

Ten Simple Steps

Evangelization is not complicated or difficult. It's essentially a matter of living your own faith and being open to sharing your faith with others. Cardinal James Hickey, re-tired archbishop of Washington, D.C., offers 10 practical things that people can do at home, at school, or at work to spread the Good News of Jesus:

- **Tip #1: Be a show-off.** "I'm not asking you to be a 'show-off' in the usual sense of that term," the cardinal says. "I am suggesting that a powerful way to spread the Good News is to demonstrate it in daily life. If your faith really affects how you speak and act in private and in public, people will take notice. A faith lived is a powerful, attractive faith!"

- **Tip #2: Help someone in need.** "Why do we admire Mother Teresa?" he asks. "Because she took Jesus at his word. She saw Jesus in the poorest of the poor. When we put our faith into action by serving those in need, our faith comes alive and has the power to attract others. So if you want to evangelize, reach out to the sick, the homebound, the troubled, the homeless, the hungry, the imprisoned. Evangelizers don't just write checks. When possible, they engage in "hands on" service to the poor. When others see this, they will start taking the faith more seriously."

- **Tip #3: Pray.** "Prayer is the 'engine' that drives evangelization," the cardinal explains. "Without prayer, we always fail in our attempts to spread the Gospel. Just think about it. Before Jesus preached, or worked a miracle, or died on the cross, He prayed. So should we. Prayer is something we can all do — anyplace, anytime. It's something we can do for ourselves and others. Make no mistake. Almost everyone — even the most hardened unbeliever — appreciates your prayers in time of need!"

- **Tip #4: Respect other people.** "Unfortunately, common courtesy isn't too common today," he says. "As followers of Jesus, we need to be more than courteous. We need to have a deep respect for the God-given dignity of each human being. Not everyone is asked to write a treatise about human dignity. But we are all called to show respect and concern for each person — those we like and those we don't. Needless to say, we're not effective evangelizers when we imagine we're better than everyone else or when we disrespect someone because of race, sex, or economic status. When we show that we respect others — by how we treat them — then we stand a much better chance of opening their minds and hearts to the Gospel."

- **Tip #5: Evangelization begins at home.** "You've heard the old saying, 'Charity begins at home.' So does evangelization," says the cardinal. "Husbands and wives should help each other take their faith seriously and grow in it. Parents are the first to help their children open their minds and hearts to Jesus by teaching them how to pray and giving them their first religion lessons. How important for parents to practice their faith — especially by participating in Mass each Sunday. How important for parents to make sure their children really learn what the Catholic faith is all about. A strong, loving, and truly Catholic home also has a good impact on the extended family."

- **Tip #6: Start with your friends.** "When evangelization moves beyond the family circle, you might start getting uncomfortable. After all, no one wants to be thought of as a 'religious fanatic.' So start with your friends," he suggests. "We all have friends who are 'unchurched' or 'barely churched.' This year, try to convince just one of them to consider or reconsider the faith. Build on that trust and love you already have with that person. Ask the Lord to provide just the right opportunity to speak to your friend about the faith."

- **Tip #7: Share your faith story.** "Wait a minute, you might be saying! My faith story? That's right! The Lord has touched the hearts of every believer with his truth and love," he explains. "So take a minute and think of the ways God has touched your life. And then write down some of the highlights so that when you're talking to family or friends about the faith, you'll be able to speak personally. Don't underestimate the power of personal testimony. People will think more seriously about the faith when you are willing to tell them what it has meant in your own life."

- **Tip #8: Include God in your everyday vocabulary.** "It's not against the law to speak about God," says the cardinal. "No one can order you to leave your faith at home when you go to work in the morning. Be conscious of God's presence in your everyday life – in decisions great and small. And don't be afraid to mention casually how God works in your life. Doing so helps us raise people's awareness that God is very much alive and present in our midst."

- **Tip #9: Proclaim Jesus.** "When a family member, friend, or colleague seems ready, speak to that person about Jesus," the cardinal urges. "You don't have to be a theologian to do this. But you must know and love Jesus. And you have to be able to express, in clear and concise terms, who he is and what he did to save us. Think of yourself as making an introduction. You do it all the time at home, at work, and in social situations. In evangelization, you are simply introducing a well-disposed person to the Lord Jesus! You are helping someone else to know the Lord Jesus who has already touched your mind and heart with his love."

- **Tip #10: Bring a friend to church.** "Some of our newly baptized people told me that they had taken this step because a friend brought them to church," he recalls. "That's good, practical evangelization. If you work downtown, ask a friendly co-worker if he or she would like to attend noon Mass with you. Invite your friends to come to Sunday Mass or a parish adult-formation class. If the children of Catholic parents in your neighborhood aren't getting to church on Sunday, offer to take them."

St. Monica Sodality

For many people, prayer will be the avenue in which they feel the most comfortable.

Father C. Frank Phillips, C.R., pastor of St. John Cantius Parish in Chicago, believed so strongly in the power of prayer that he started St. Monica Sodality for people who have a loved one away from the Church. At the first meeting, 30 people gathered to pray a novena to St. Monica, who is credited with the conversion of her son, St. Augustine. Today, hundreds of people attend the monthly prayer service in Chicago, and many more have formed chapters of St. Monica Sodality throughout the world. Members have the consolation of knowing they are not alone. They have also seen impressive results.

"The oldest person we had return was an 86-year-old woman who returned after a lapse of 60 years," Father Phillips recalls. "Another couple prayed for their two sons, who finally came to Midnight Mass with them on Christmas, and then continued to come to Mass each week. One month later, the father died, but he had the joy of seeing his family reconciled."

Prayer allows you to shift the burden into God's hands. "I was estranged from my daughter," one man recalls. "I felt so sad that it must have shown. One day when I was filling my truck with gas, an African-American woman came up to me and said, 'You just have to give it to the Lord.' Then she went back to her car and left. Deep down I knew she was right. So I let go of the pain of not seeing my daughter and my grandchildren. Several months later, my daughter called and I saw my grandchildren for the first time. Many times God draws straight with a crooked line. We just have to have faith and be the beacon that shows our children the way home."

"I say this prayer very often, because it is a prayer of complete trust in God: 'I cannot solve this, Lord, but into thy hands I commend my spirit.' To me, the fact that Jesus, dying on the cross, prayed that prayer gives it a very special significance."

— Cardinal Basil Hume, O.S.B.

At the Cross with Mary

Father Ronald Rolheiser, O.M.I., points out that there are times when there is truly nothing you can do except pray. "All of us know the feeling of standing in a situation and being powerless, at least in that we are helpless to change anything practically," he says. "What can we do when faced with that? Nothing — except live with the powerlessness, carry the tension, try to transmute it into something else, and wait for a new day, a day of new opportunity for resolution of the pain."

He uses as an example the image of Our Lady at the foot of the cross.

"All Scripture tells us is that Mary stood there," he says. "Standing, however, connoted strength. Thus, even in the face of the crucifixion, she was strong, not prostrate in helplessness (as artists sometimes depict her). And what's she saying? Nothing. Mary said not a single word; not, I suspect, because she didn't want to protest, but because there wasn't anything that she could have said at that moment that would have made any difference. Under the cross, she was powerless both in that there was not a single thing she could do to stop the crucifixion and in that she was just as helpless to protest her son's innocence. Hence, she's not standing under the cross protesting to the bystanders, trying to explain her view of things. She's powerless. Silent. There's no protest. All she can do is ponder, that is, hold the tension, stand silently amidst the misunderstanding, bigotry, and jealousy and, in that, try to gestate its opposite — understanding, compassion, and love."

The idea of standing silently seems foreign to our nature. We want to solve problems. We want to fix things that are broken. We want to find answers to the questions. We want to take away the pain. When we stand silently, however, we allow God to work through the situation.

"We are too hard on ourselves because of our inadequacies," Father Rolheiser says. "In many of the most intimate and painful situations of our lives, we are precisely not able to fix things, be adequate,

"We must never seek to leave the foot of the cross sooner than God would have us do."

— VENERABLE CHARLES DE FOUCAULD

or redeem the situation. Sometimes there's nothing to be done . . . but nothing can be enough, as it was for Mary, under the cross. Sometimes all we can do is stand silently, in strength, bearing an unbearable tension, waiting for our hearts to do something our actions can't, namely, transmute confusion into insight, anger into blessing, and hatred into love."

Most people will agree that there is a reason for everything. If we believe St. Paul, then we believe "that in everything God works for good with those who love him, who are called according to his purpose" (Rom 8:28). When a loved one leaves the Church, it is really not your problem. It's God's problem. Giving the situation to God and constantly striving toward unconditional love, in spite of your pain, in spite of your fears, in spite of your questions and your concerns, may be precisely what God is asking you to do.

Chapter Notes

Cardinal James Hickey . . . offers 10 practical things . . .: Cardinal James Hickey, "Ten Tips for Practical Evangelization," Archdiocese of Washington, *www.adw.org/evangel/evan_index.html*.

"All of us know the feeling of standing in a situation and being powerless . . .": Ronald Rolheiser, O.M.I., "Doing Nothing Is Sometimes Enough," *Western Catholic Reporter* (May 15, 2000).

"All Scripture tells us is that Mary stood there . . .": Ibid.

Resources

Programs and Information for Fallen-Away Catholics

Come Home
Diocese of Buffalo
Communications Department
Catholic Center
795 Main St.
Buffalo, NY 14203
(716) 847-8719

Landings
Joan A. Horn, National Coordinator
3311 Big Bend
Austin, TX 78731
(512) 452-7566
e-mail: *horn@mail.utexas.edu*

Paulist National Catholic Evangelization
3031 Fourth St., NE
Washington, DC 20017
(202) 832-5022
www.paulist.org/pncea

ReMembering
North American Forum on the Catechumenate
7715 Leesburg Pike, Suite 308
Falls Church, VA 22043

Books for Questioning and Fallen-Away Catholics

Annulment: Do You Have a Case? by Terence E. Tierney, Joseph J. Campo (Contributor) (Alba House, 1993).

Annulment: Your Chance to Remarry within the Catholic Church, by Joseph P. Swack (Harper San Francisco, 1983).

Beyond Gay, by David Morrison (Our Sunday Visitor Books, 1999).

Could You Ever Come Back to the Catholic Church? by Lorene Hanley Duquin (Alba House, 1997).

The Holy Longing: The Search for a Christian Spirituality, by Ronald Rolheiser (Doubleday, 1999).

How to Survive Being Married to a Catholic, by Michael Henesy and Rosemary Gallagher (Liguori Publications, 1997).

Lost and Found Catholics, by Christopher M. Bellitto (St. Anthony Messenger Press, 1999).

One Hundred Answers to Your Questions on Annulments, by Edward N. Peters (Ginn Press, 1997).

Prove It! God, by Amy Welborn (Our Sunday Visitor Books, 2000).

The Return of the Prodigal Son, by Henri J. Nouwen (Doubleday, 1992).

While You Were Gone: A Handbook for Returning Catholics, by William J. Bausch (Twenty-third Publications, 1994).

Why Do Catholics Do That? By Kevin Orlin Johnson, Ph.D. (Ballantine Books, 1994).

Testimonies of Catholic Converts

Born Fundamentalist, Born Again Catholic, by David B. Currie (Ignatius Press, 1996).

By What Authority? An Evangelical Discovers Catholic Tradition, by Mark P. Shea (Our Sunday Visitor Books, 1996).

Could You Ever Become a Catholic? by Lorene Hanley Duquin (Alba House, 2001).

Crossing the Tiber, by Stephen K. Ray (Ignatius Press, 1997).

Journeys Home, by Marcus C. Grodi, M.Div. (Queenship Publishing, 1997).

Rome Sweet Home: Our Journey to Catholicism, by Scott and Kimberly Hahn (Ignatius Press, 1993).

Surprised by Truth, by Patrick Madrid (Basilica Press, 1994).

Surprised by Truth 2, by Patrick Madrid (Sophia Press, 2000).

General Reference Books for Families and Friends

Addiction & Grace, by Gerald G. May, M.D. (Harper & Row, 1988).

Anti-Catholicism in American Culture, by Robert P. Lockwood (Our Sunday Visitor Books, 2000).

Catechism of the Catholic Church, Second Edition (United States Catholic Conference — Libreria Editrice Vaticana, 2000; available from Our Sunday Visitor Books).

Catholic and Christian, by Alan Schreck (Servant Books, 1984).

Co-Dependent No More, by Melody Beattie (Harper & Row, 1987).

Healing the Shame that Binds You, by John Bradshaw (Health Communications, Inc., 1988).

The How-To Book of Catholic Devotions, by Mike Aquilina and Regis J. Flaherty (Our Sunday Visitor Books, 2000).

The Marginal Catholic: Challenge, Don't Crush, by Joseph M. Champlin (Ave Maria Press, 1989).

Mention Your Request Here: The Church's Most Powerful Novenas, by Michael Dubruiel (Our Sunday Visitor Books, 2000).

The Next American Spirituality: Finding God in the Twenty-first Century, by George Gallup, Jr., and Timothy Jones (Cook Communications Ministries, 2000).

Ordinary Suffering of Extraordinary Saints, by Vincent J. O'Malley, C.M. (Our Sunday Visitor Books, 2000).

Praying Our Goodbyes, by Joyce Rupp, O.S.M. (Ave Maria Press, 1988).

Saintly Companions, by Vincent J. O'Malley, C.M. (Alba House, 1995).

Shadows of the Heart: A Spirituality of the Negative Emotions, by James D. Whitehead and Evelyn Eaton Whitehead (Crossroad Publishing Company, 1994).

Surveying the Religious Landscape, by George Gallup, Jr., and D. Michael Lindsay (Morehouse Publishing, 1999).

What Catholics Really Believe, by Karl Keating (Ignatius Press, 1992).

Support and Information for Families and Friends

AFF American Family Foundation
Cult Information Services
P.O. Box 2265
Bonita Springs, FL 34133
(941) 514-3081
fax: (941) 514-3451
e-mail: *admin2@csj.org*
www.csj.org/index.htm

Al-Anon Family Group Headquarters, Inc.
1600 Corporate Landing Parkway
Virginia Beach, VA 23454
1-888-4AL-ANON

Alcoholics Anonymous World Services
Grand Central Station
P.O. Box 459
New York, NY 10163
(212) 870-3400
www.alcoholics-anonymous.org

Family Life Center International
P.O. Box 6060
Port Charlotte, FL 33949
(941) 764-7725
email: *sjck@sunline.net*
www.familylifecenter.net

St. Monica Sodality
825 N. Carpenter St.
Chicago, IL 60622
(312) 243-7373

Websites

Author's Website (Lorene Hanley Duquin)
www.couldyouever.homepage.com

Barna Research Online
www.barna.org

Catholic Answers Homepage
www.catholic.com

Catholic-Pages
www.catholic-pages.com

Catholic Web Directory
www.saintfrancis.net/links.htm

Coming Home Network
www.chnetwork.org

Mirror of Truth
www.mirroroftruth.org

National Conference of Catholic Bishops
www.nccbuscc.org

Our Sunday Visitor, Inc. (*The Catholic Answer* magazine)
www.osv.com

Reveal (cult awareness and education)
www.reveal.org

St. Joseph's Covenant Keepers (an online resource for Catholic dads)
www.dads.org

Our Sunday Visitor. . .
Your Source for Discovering the Riches of the Catholic Faith

Our Sunday Visitor has an extensive line of materials for young children, teens, and adults. Our books, Bibles, booklets, CD-ROMs, audios, and videos are available in bookstores worldwide.

To receive a FREE full-line catalog or for more information, call **Our Sunday Visitor** at **1-800-348-2440**. Or write, **Our Sunday Visitor** / 200 Noll Plaza / Huntington, IN 46750.

- -

Please send me: ___A catalog
Please send me materials on:

___Apologetics and catechetics	___Reference works
___Prayer books	___Heritage and the saints
___The family	___The parish

Name_____

Address_____Apt._____

City_____State_____Zip_____

Telephone (   ) _____

A13BBABP

- -

Please send a friend: ___A catalog
Please send a friend materials on:

____Apologetics and catechetics	____Reference works
____Prayer books	____Heritage and the saints
____The family	____The parish

Name_____

Address_____Apt._____

City_____State_____Zip_____

Telephone (   ) _____

A13BBABP

- -

Our Sunday Visitor
200 Noll Plaza
Huntington, IN 46750
Toll free: 1-800-348-2440
E-mail: osvbooks@osv.com
Website: www.osv.com